FLIPPED

FLIPPED

How Bottom-up Co-creation Is Replacing
Top-down Innovation

JOHN WINSOR

CHICAGO

Copyright © 2004, 2010 John Winsor
All rights reserved. No part of this book may be reproduced or transmitted in any form or by any means, electronic or mechanical, including photocopying, recording, or by any information storage and retrieval system, without express written permission from the publisher.

Printed in the United States.

Library of Congress Cataloging-in-Publication Data

Winsor, John, 1959-
 Flipped : how bottom-up co-creation is replacing top-down innovation / John Winsor.
   p. cm.
 Rev. ed. of: Beyond the brand : why engaging the right customers is essential to winning in business. 2004
 Summary: "Advertising leader John Winsor discusses how companies can use 'co-creation' tools to create new products, services, and marketing strategies in collaboration with their customers"--Provided by publisher.
 ISBN-13: 978-1-932841-48-0 (pbk.)
 ISBN-10: 1-932841-48-2 (pbk.)
 1. Product management. 2. Brand loyalty. 3. Diffusion of innovations. 4. New products. 5. Marketing. I. Winsor, John, 1959- Beyond the brand. II. Title.
 HF5415.15.W565 2010
 658.8--dc22
                          2010002392
10 12 13 14   10 9 8 7 6 5 4 3 2 1

B2 Books is an imprint of Agate Publishing. Agate books are available in bulk at discount prices. For more information, go to agatepublishing.com.

For Bridget, Charlie, and Harry: The best teachers.

Table of Contents

	Acknowledgments	8
	Executive Summary	10
CHAPTER 1	Co-creating from the Bottom-Up	18
CHAPTER 2	Step One: Focus on Key Voices	36
CHAPTER 3	Step Two: Get the Story	50
CHAPTER 4	Step Three: Listen	68
CHAPTER 5	Step Four: Find Inspiration	82
CHAPTER 6	Step Five: Hone Your Intuition	94
CHAPTER 7	Step Six: Find the Center of Gravity	106
CHAPTER 8	Step Seven: Tell the Story	124

Acknowledgments

As an experiment in crowdsourcing, I placed the manuscript of *Flipped* on a wiki from the good folks at PBWorks.com. (Thanks, guys.) I then asked the crowd to help edit the book. It was a wonderful process. While a lot of folks helped out with the editing, many people also offered moral support and some great examples. I extend sincere thanks to:

Brad Noble, Alain Thys, Alex Ames, Ally Polly, Anita Lobo, Asher Adelman, Barry Polley, Ben Kaufman, Ben Malbon, Gerard Blokdijk, Bob Weil, Brandon Berger, Brett Macfarlane, Christopher Caen, Conrad Lisco, Dave Hampton, David Cary, David Friedman, David Wiggs, Dennis Bernhard, Diego Otero, Dragos Lupascu, Edward Boches, Ed Markey, Ellie Banwell, Eugene Chung, Ewan Adams, Gareth Kay, Ginger Conrad, Graham Furlong, Helen Walters, Jacob McNulty, Jeff Howe, John B. Winsor, Joseph Rueter, Jane Tabachnick, Justin McCammon, Karen LaBerdia, Kathy Huynh, Mark Earls, Matti Copeland, Nick Gundry, Nikki Kauffman, Noah Robinson, Oliver Wright, Pam Markhall, Paul McConaughy, Peter Thomson, Philip Tribe, Lilly Evans, Regan Mead, Robb Shurr, Rohit Nand, Scott Gwozdz, Sean Net, Doug Seibold, Scott Karambis, Shaun Abrahamson, Abbey Smith, Scott Prindle, Steve Tennant, Tate Linden, Warren Ng, Wayne Addy, Wendy Dembo, Wesley

Robison, Luke Wicker, Zack Grossbart, Walter Knapp, Peter Majarich, Koert Bakker, Heather Lefevre, K. Hayes, PB Ferrigan, J. McKeown, Kelley Troia, S. O'Brien, V. Subramaniam.

Executive Summary

In 2003 when I first wrote this book, then entitled, *Beyond the Brand*, the idea of flipping the innovation paradigm from being top-down and inside out to becoming co-creative from the bottom-up was a trend that hadn't really caught on. Sure, Friendster was all the rage, the open source movement that started with Linux software was just getting off the ground, and Wikipedia was just a glimmer in Jimmy Wale's eye. My, how things have changed.

The power of co-creation has gone from a sideshow at the circus, mostly existing on the far end of the Long Tail, to an indispensible tool that affects all companies. If you are still trying to use top-down tools to drive innovation, you only need to look as far as General Motors to realize that the command and control style of innovation doesn't work.

To survive today, every CEO and CMO has to allow their customers to participate in their brands. Brands are becoming Petri dishes that are only a platform for a dialogue between the company and its customers. If the company is willing to give up control and allow co-creation to happen, from the bottom-up not only will they get to know their customers better, they will also build deeper trust from which more innovative products and marketing can be created that connect more intimately with them. In today's turbulent market, who doesn't want the ability to have more loyal customers?

WHAT GETS IN THE WAY?

Even though this is a common goal, businesses have long lived under the pretense that the world in which we live is controllable. The language of business – "plan," "budget," "target" – contributes to this illusion. How did this come to be? Encouraged by the promises of the scientific revolution, businesses operated under the belief that, with the right systems and controls, anything could be accomplished. After all, this was the same age that put man on the moon.

In reality, companies are a lot like frogs. Do you know the best way to cook a frog? The frog gets cooked when the water it sits in starts out cool and the temperature only changes one degree at a time. The frog does not have the subtle sensory skills to see and feel its environment change. This same thing often happens to established companies. The external environment may change slowly – but if companies fail to notice that change, they're dead in the water. Entrepreneurial companies have an easier time adapting because they have more mobility and can react to changes more quickly. These companies act more like a live frog put into boiling water. They can immediately feel the radical difference in the environment and jump out of harm's way. Established companies that have been historically successful have a very difficult time jumping at all, even out of boiling water. Even when they do recognize a temperature difference, they are rendered immobile by their stubborn dependence on existing systems. Instead, they choose to remain under the delusion that they can control the temperature of the water.

The events of the last decade have challenged this notion of control in significant ways. We've become perfectly accustomed to media stories about some of the most successful companies in the world fighting for their very survival. In a matter of half a decade, the environment in which these businesses were able to prosper for the past half-century or more has changed beyond recognition.

One of the problems is that marketing has been appropriated as a distorted form of communication in which the company always assumes the position of power and is not necessarily required to either listen or respond to feedback. People are expected to sit quietly and listen; many react to this by tuning out much of what is said. They are developing a Brand Immune System: the reality is that people will only pay attention to your brand or product when they actually need or want your product or service – not before, and usually not after. Most companies have failed to stay engaged in the ever-evolving lives of their customers, making it impossible for them to notice the subtleties of the two-way conversation (if they're allowing it in the first place). When they stop paying attention, customers will also disconnect from the relationship. But maintaining this relationship can be both profitable and potentially more defensible in today's competitive marketplace.

Companies spend too much of their time, energy, and money using top-down tools to innovate, rather than finding out what is relevant to their customers from the bottom-up. Likewise, many companies outsource their most important relationship – the one with their customers – giving someone else full control to attempt to understand their customers by using traditional top-down tools in their often static and tightly controlled conversations.

One tool that has supported innovation is market research. Traditional market research is based upon the belief that through the effort of gathering vast amounts of consumer data, a marketer can automatically gain a deep understanding of who people are. While massive data files, sorted by powerful computers, can yield interesting information on where and when people shop, it fails to reveal why they behave the way they do. Part of the problem is the assumption that more is better and that statistical verifiability is what matters. While a large number of responses can be interesting, many studies have shown that a couple dozen customers can yield the same answers as several hundred. The biggest issue with becoming too reliant on quantitative tools is the reality that people answer only the question that is asked. What happens when the question is wrong?

Another top-down tool that dominates the conversation between companies and their customers is the focus group. While companies spend over $1 billion on focus groups, some basic flaws plague this methodology. First, they are conducted in facilities that strip away the context of the customer's life. How can anyone talk about the experience of driving a car without sitting in a car seat and talking about it in the context of the activity? Other issues, such as groupthink and bullying among focus group participants, only compound the problems with focus groups. How do you take eight people out of the context of their lives and spend two hours in a strange environment, trying to cover ten topics? This gives each participant only a couple of minutes to react. How can you make significant strategic decisions after only getting to know a person for a couple of minutes? Can you really use this information to design a product or marketing campaign that expresses a deep understanding of your customers' needs, and space that allows space for them to co-create?

When companies concentrate primarily on increasing their sales by using static top-down techniques, with only a secondary hope of developing deeper relationships with their customers, no agency or consultant can benefit them in the long term. To enact real bottom-up change in the marketplace, companies must incorporate their use of consultants and agencies, as partners, to help shape their brands and products based on their customers' wants and needs. They must intimately know their customers at the front end of the process, not only as an afterthought. This ongoing engagement allows the essential space for co-creation.

The bottom line is that an intimate relationship with your customers has to begin *before* you offer them a product, brand, or service.

Their insights, needs, and desires should be driving production from the bottom-up at the front end, and sales thereafter.

TOO MANY CHOICES, NOT ENOUGH TIME

With too many tangible offerings, people create filters and use other tools, like social media, to make sense of the many messages they're bombarded with every day. In every category of business there are more product choices than anyone could ever try, let alone purchase. No matter how much branding or advertising a company does, it's increasingly difficult to wade through the clutter. Studies have demonstrated that providing *too many* options – particularly when the real distinctions between them are small (there are over three dozen different flavors of Crest Toothpaste, for example) – can cause people to feel overwhelmed and overloaded, and as a result, less likely to pursue *any* of the options available. People want variety, but they want companies to be reasonable at the same time. When the products available to them are relevant to their needs and their lifestyles, customers will feel that those companies have actually done their homework. Throwing out dozens of choices and assuming people will find something they like doesn't foster intimacy between companies and their customers. People don't necessarily need more choices; they need choices that are personally relevant. The reality is that in response to this product overload, people are suggesting that more isn't always better; that perhaps quality – or at least relevance – is more important than quantity. The only possible exception to this way of thinking is in people's ongoing quest to somehow find more *time*.

Articles in the 1960s and '70s used to talk about the rise of leisure time we would experience by the year 2000 because of the promise of productivity following the development of technologies like the computer. What happened? Remember how many futurists accepted the notion of a four-day workweek as the norm for most of us at the turn of the century? What happened? With our infinite choices, from

500 television channels to 125,000 new books every year, we've filled up our "extra" time pretty fast.

If there is one constant for all of us it is our lack of time, whether real or perceived. I look at it this way: I'm 49. The average American male lives to be 77.8 years old (according to the National Center For Health Statistics). That's 28,397 days, so I've got about 10,512 days left. If you're like me, you: sleep eight hours per day (if you're lucky) – 3,565 days; eat for two and a half hours per day – 1,114 days; spend half an hour per day in the bathroom (hot showers rule!) – 223 days; work eight hours per day (16 years, maybe, maybe not) – 1,927 days; work out one hour per day (hopefully) – 446 days; commute one hour per day (at least) – 446 days; hang out with the family two hours per day – 892 days; do things you don't really want to do one hour per day (pay bills, listen to telemarketers, do yard work) – 446 days. That leaves 1,453 days, or about one hour per day, left for following your bliss. I don't know about you, but anyone hoping to get my attention these days better make it really mean something to me, especially if it infringes on that one sacred hour.

POWER TO THE PEOPLE

People today expect the ability to co-create and lead innovation, forcing companies to devise creative solutions to be competitive in this new bottom-up age. Such an environment generates opportunities for companies that are creative and intimately listen to the cultures they are involved with; joining forces with other creatives including artists, journalists, filmmakers and musicians to create new ways of expression and creation. The resulting products that demonstrate a real understanding of their customers in the context of their lives will be successful. Instead of thinking globally and acting locally, the successful philosophy will be to think locally and act globally.

In the vast middle of the market, people will continue to treat brands as resources. These people do not have the time or the energy to be proactive in developing their own, relevant products. Instead, they will allow their peers to do most of the heavy lifting in creating new cultural materials – and then adopt those products as their own. Brands that connect with people's imaginations, that inspire, provoke and stimulate, that help them interpret the world that surrounds them, will be successful. Brands that are able to make the transition to providing honest, original, cultural materials, offering space for co-creation, will win. Proactive people will carefully weed out and broadcast those products, and companies, that they do not trust. Many companies have already discovered that being good corporate citizens can be good for their brands. In this new era, it's the creative citizens of a community – the people and the brands – that will help companies survive by co-creating from the bottom-up.

CATCH THE WAVE

A few years ago, I sold the company I had owned for ten years, Sports & Fitness Publishing, and took an extended sabbatical. I went to Mexico to learn how to surf. Surfing has taught me that there is no substitution for repetitive practice. Many of the lessons I've learned from the sport of surfing are at the core of this book. Surfing is one of the iconic alternative sports representing not only the youth culture but also the beach culture. Many companies have used surfing to leverage their brands into household names in every town across the country. Everybody loves the image of surfing. Yet, I've discovered there are very few people who actually surf. Why is that? There is one simple answer: surfing is hard. I have a personal theory about surfing. It takes riding a thousand waves to become a surfer. It doesn't matter if you catch 20 waves a day for 50 days or one wave a day for a thousand days; you just can't get around the experience of learning the hard way.

Just as in surfing, there is no substitution for one thousand waves, or in this case, a thousand personal interactions with your customer. I know it seems like an overwhelming number, but there is just no way around it. Mastering the seven steps above takes lots of practice.

And practice will give you the chance to develop your own style of engaging in a bottom-up strategy with your customers and the marketplace, giving you the opportunity to drive real innovation.

Thriving in this new bottom-up economy is a journey. There are no quick answers, just wonderful learning experiences.

CHAPTER 1
Co-creating from the Bottom-Up

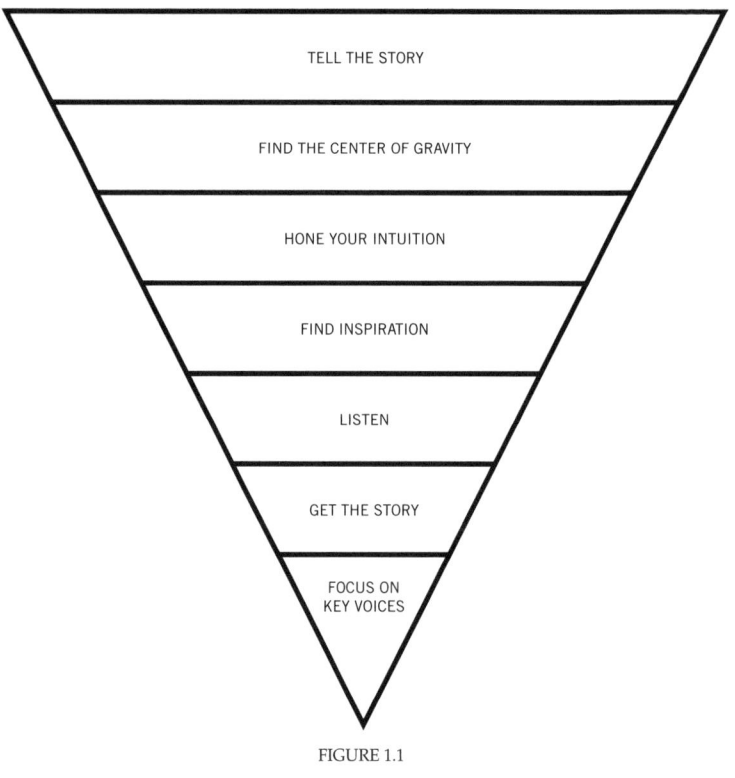

FIGURE 1.1

Many things have contributed to the declining effectiveness of top-down marketing and innovation tools. Access to the Internet has led to rapid improvements in technology and radical changes in customer's behavior. This tremendous increase in information available gives customers the ability to choose products from far further afield than ever before and to discuss the relative merits, comparing with competitors. Customers are now able to act as consumers, producers and critics. People now have greater freedom, access to vast amounts of information, and more choices than ever before, but they have too little time to research everything they buy and are less willing to purchase from companies that are not prepared to engage them in a dialogue.

This challenge to companies to bring the right customers directly into the planning process is compounded by changes in the environment in which brands exist. Everything from unstable macro-economic conditions, disruptive technologies, and new competitors rising from nowhere will continue to threaten companies that remain disconnected from their customers and their communities. Additional factors, including the rising power of retailers and the prevalence of fear, interject still more uncertainty into the marketing and innovation processes. This uncertainty is difficult to predict or prepare for. The only way to deal with it is to accept its presence and actively work to gain a deeper understanding of the environments in which brands work. Brands must continually strive to act like a local merchant, like a citizen of the community. In a true community, participants share their personal experiences. If companies want to identify with and be relevant to their customers, they must first become trusted, committed community members. Only then can they begin the journey towards creating long-term sustainable relationships.

Most of us have been trained to think that there is always a "right way" to do things, and we often try to impose that perspective on our customers and business members. There's been a story cruising around the Internet about how out of touch American businessmen can be with their environments.

The story goes that an American businessman had just sold his business and was taking some time to think about his next business opportunity. He decided to head south and spend the season in a coastal Mexican village. One day, he was standing at the pier thinking about his next business move when a small boat with just one fisherman aboard docked at the pier. Inside the small boat were several large yellow fin tuna. The American complimented the Mexican on the quality of his fish and asked how long it took to catch them. The Mexican replied it was only a little while. The American then asked why he didn't stay out longer and catch more fish? The Mexican said he had enough to support his family's immediate needs. The American then asked, "But what do you do with the rest of your time?" The Mexican fisherman said, "I sleep late, fish a little, play with my children, take a siesta with my wife, Maria, then stroll into the village each evening where I sip wine and play guitar with my *amigos*... I have a full and busy life, *señor*." The American scoffed, "I am a Harvard MBA. I've just sold my company for millions, and I can help you. You should spend more time fishing, and with the proceeds buy a bigger boat. With the proceeds from the bigger boat you could buy several boats, until eventually you would have a fleet of fishing boats. Instead of selling your catch to a middleman, you would sell directly to the processor, eventually opening your own cannery. You would control the product, processing and distribution. You would need to leave this small coastal fishing village and move to Mexico City, then Los Angeles and eventually New York City where you will run your expanding enterprise." The Mexican fisherman asked, "But *señor*, how long will this all take?" To which the American replied, "Not long. Maybe 15 to 20 years." "But what then, *señor*?" asked the fisherman. The American laughed and said, "That's the best part. When the time is right you announce an Initial Public Offering, sell your company stock to the public and become very rich. You would make millions." "Millions, *señor*? Then what?" asked the fisherman. The American said, "Then you would retire, and move to a small coastal fishing village where you would sleep late, fish a little, play with your kids, take a siesta with your wife, then stroll to the village in the evenings where you could sip wine and play guitar with your *amigos*."

While this Mexican fisherman isn't a customer of the average American businessman, he acts very much like most customers do. They're living their own lives without staying up at night thinking about which laundry detergent brand will make them a better person or more popular with their friends. Yet, in the context of the businessman's world, a customer is just that – a customer – rather than a person. Many brands today are disconnected from their communities and customers. But these same companies act surprised when their customers get upset and suggest that they seem out of touch.

CHANGE AND LEARNING

In turbulent times, many companies act like deer caught in the headlights of an oncoming car. It is hard for companies to break their habits and shift gears to be proactive in the face of change. Like people, companies resist change with tenacity, yet the changing environment and customer needs require – or demand – that the corporate status quo must adapt. In order to engage their customers, companies must place their brand within a deeper context of their customer's lives.

Many times, companies get so wrapped up in finding that right way to connect with their customers that they lose touch with their communities and become defined by their own self-imposed boundaries from a lack of connectivity. They must broaden their view and understand that they are part of a larger community. A community is defined by its collective dialogue and, hence, has no boundaries. Instead, communities have horizons – a place one never quite reaches. It is not a boundary or a goal. It is not defined as a final destination, but more as a relative journey. Companies must recognize that in order to deal with the uncertainty that the world presents they must strive to jump into the community – like the Mexican fishing village – and enjoy the central experience of being part of that community. By doing so, companies can develop more profitable long-term sustainable relationships built on mutual trust and understanding.

How can businesses accomplish this? Well, it starts with creativity. Creativity can be found in anyone who is prepared to enjoy the journey of interacting in a community. They must be willing to get out of their offices and use their curiosity to rediscover the reality of the communities in which they live from the bottom-up. Companies must take the time to wonder. Introducing creativity and wonder means that they must strive to live by more human values, like honesty, friendship, and empathy. It means that companies must reframe and recontextualize their current worldview. They must be willing to take the leap of faith, try and fail, and, most of all, use a bottom-up strategy to learn and become competitive in today's dynamic world.

DEVELOPING YOUR BOTTOM-UP STRATEGY

Many companies focus their strategic thinking around current market needs by getting into a conference room and divining the future (or attempting to). It's a very inside-out, or top-down, approach. In a reversal of this traditional process, exceptional companies use an outside-in approach, or bottom-up strategy, to engage in a dialogue with the other members of their community, allowing them to co-create innovations with their customers. This holistic, organic strategy allows companies to continually recontextualize and reframe their brand, making necessary adjustments as the community and customers evolve.

I heard an interesting story while in New York, talking with an account planner at a prestigious global advertising agency. He said that throughout the advertising industry, clients are often nervous about relying solely on the intuition of the creative teams at the agencies they use. Thus, many of them direct their agencies to "be creative" and propose a few new concepts; then clients test these ideas on their "customers" using focus groups. Since most clients strive for an efficient process, their agency's creative concepts are sent off to the same focus group facilities and moderators, using the same respondents from the same databases, as everyone else in the industry. It's no surprise that clients get nearly identical answers. While companies recognize the value of intuition and creativity in their planning processes, most are unprepared to jump all the way into a radically new way of thinking. However, asking for a "second opinion" in a completely different context – like the focus group – does as much damage as not being creative at the front end of the process.

Most strategy based solely on traditional research methods is in trouble. As practiced today, most strategy works *against* creativity and the kind of risk-taking that is crucial to creating innovative products and services. Its typical pattern, as shown in Fig. 1.1 on page 18, is linear. This makes sense in highly logical and predictable situations. But a company's strategy needs to be contextual and open. It has to be human. Hence, a bottom-up strategy considers these factors. The strategizing pattern is shown in Fig. 1.2 (see page 24). It's a perpetual cycle.

So what is a bottom-up strategy, really? In many ways, the concept mirrors the computer software industry's idea of open source development, which is usually linked to Linus Torvalds and the development of the Linux operating system.

A bottom-up strategy takes the open source philosophy a step

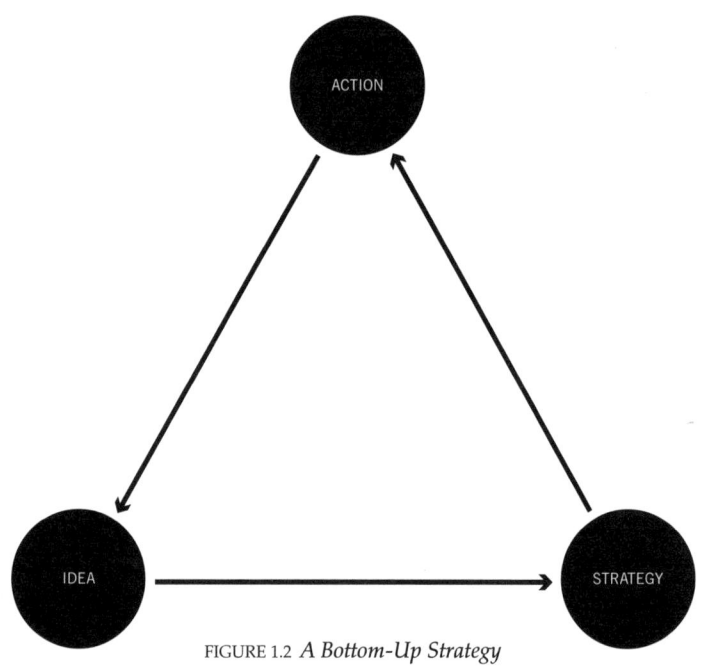

FIGURE 1.2 *A Bottom-Up Strategy*

further. First, it's about loosening the control over the strategic process and focusing on guiding it instead of owning it. It's about inviting the right customers, suppliers, and employees to participate in an open, informed process based on solid guiding principles. To do this well, companies must focus their strategic energies on building consensus and communities. The focus has to be on the quality of the input into the strategy and the communications of those ideas to the community. Companies must focus on being evolutionary.

Disruptive innovation fueled by bottom-up learning means companies must participate in an open way within their community. This requires true corporate transparency, in everything from marketing to manufacturing, and a more long-term, sustainable outlook of their community.

Companies that are able to make the transition to providing honest, original, culturally relevant materials and products will win. People will carefully weed out and broadcast to their peers those companies and brands that they do not trust. Many companies have discovered that being deeply connected to their community is good for their brands. In this new era, brands will have to become good, *creative* citizens of the community in order to survive.

In the context of the rapidly changing business environment, it is time to question what we already know, and how we attempt to learn what we don't. Are we using tools that provide us with meaningful and useful insights that can drive corporate strategy from the context of our customers, bottom-up through the organization? Can data be transformed, from the bottom-up instead of top-down, into relevant innovation? The only solution is to develop new ways of understanding and finding meaning in the dynamic flux.

L > C

The principle that learning has to be greater than or equal to change is at the core of a bottom-up strategy. The one constant in these turbulent times is that change is happening faster than ever; thus, learning has to happen even more quickly. Part of the learning process requires knowing what to do with the intelligence you acquire; this is the step that facilitates real change. This idea may seem quite simple, yet it may be challenging to many people who have traditionally been involved in product development.

While learning has always needed to be greater than change in order for a company to grow, the rate of this change has accelerated from the old business environment, where change occurred gradually, during a decade or over the course of someone's career. Today, change seems to happen overnight. One day you are ahead of the pack, and the very next day, you are struggling to keep up. This means that the rate of learning has to be greater in order for any company to survive. So what do you do? With more information available, people have to acknowledge that what they perceive as being the whole picture is only a small slice of reality. Any company's world can be segmented into three areas: what we know, what we *know* we don't know, and what we *don't* know we don't know (see Fig. 1.3).

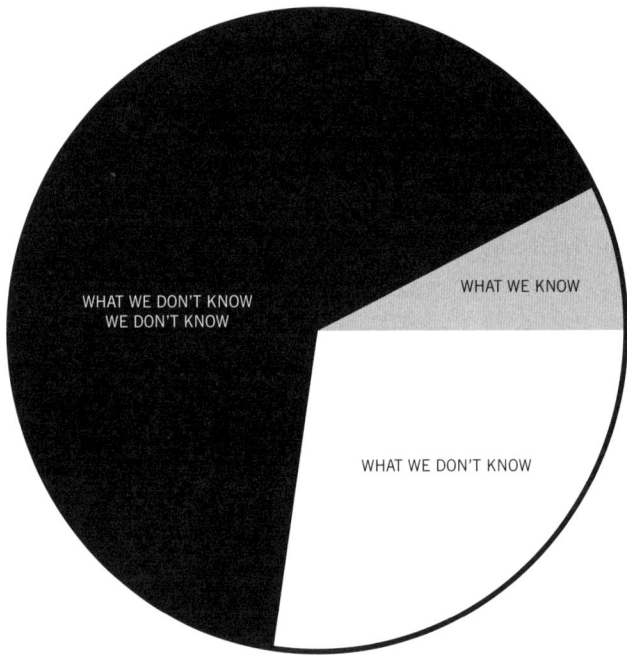

FIGURE 1.3 *The Whole Picture*

One of the problems that we all face in today's dynamic world is that the area of *what we don't know we don't know* cannot be blissfully ignored, due to its disruptive potential. Companies need to recognize this segment of their world and try to reduce it, using inspiration from the bottom-up.

Businesses often approach strategic planning as a very top-down, rigid process; even the language they use is far too structured and solemn. Planning, in its nature, requires an acceptance of the unknown and receptiveness to new ideas. Unfortunately, many companies' reaction to an influx of new information is to fall into the "paralysis by analysis" syndrome. Other companies react by panicking and making important decisions *too* quickly. The ideal solution, but one that's not easily accepted by most companies, is to rely more heavily on intuition. This is a huge paradigm shift for most businesses. People need bottom-up tools that give them the confidence to rely on their intuition when exploring the world. Businesses need fast, "real," and connected ways of making meaning of their quickly changing realities. The goal of *Flipped* is to help you build your own set of bottom-up tools, giving you the ability to develop relevant innovation faster. Inspiration developed using a bottom-up strategy can give a company the confidence needed to drive real innovation.

Bottom-up learning demands that companies are prepared to make serious mistakes when exploring their communities with their customers. It means that people inside companies need to be spontaneous, unconditioned, and expressive, and not intimidated, in these explorations. Companies need to be allowed the space to revel and learn from their stories and be creative in their interactions with other community members.

THE SEARCH FOR MEANING (OR, WHY MORE AND MORE DATA IS NOT ENOUGH)

Access to information has leveled the playing field; now everyone can obtain the same data. So how do you transform that data into relevant innovation? In such a competitive environment, what can you do to stay ahead of the competition? Once we've identified what we do (and do not) know, another crucial step must be taken. Companies must actively develop these bottom-up tools to understand and transform information into action. To find meaning in what they learn about their customers, they must identify what keeps the community balanced. By deeply understanding this center of gravity, any company can drive *relevant* innovation for their customers more quickly, without spending time or energy going in the wrong direction.

Information really exists along a continuum, with one step leading to the next.

The continuum typically looks something like this:

DATA — INFORMATION—KNOWLEDGE — INSIGHT

The problem with the information model above is that three important steps are usually left out. The goal is to drive innovation. With these three steps added to the continuum, it looks more like this (see Fig. 1.4):

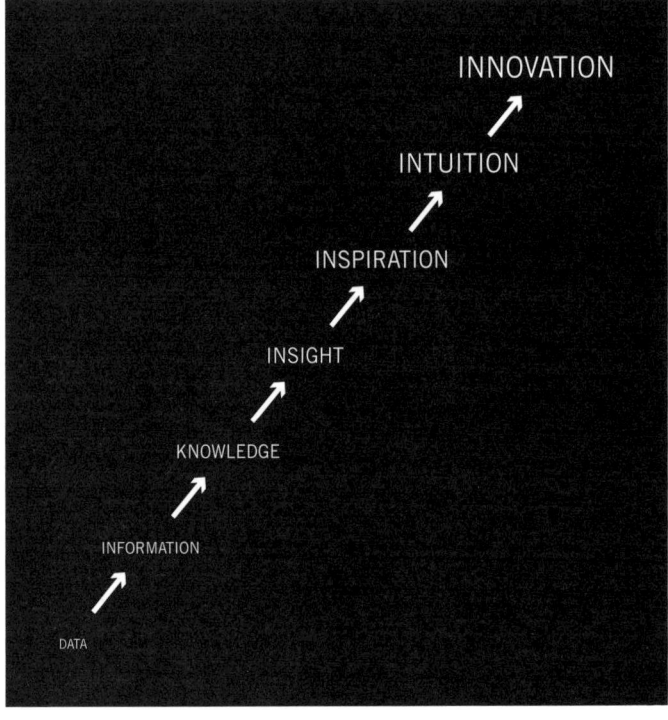

FIGURE 1.4 *The Full Information Continuum*

As Einstein said: "Any fool can know, the point is to understand." So many times, the act of knowing is based on a quick observation: "I know Joe," versus a deeper connection: "I understand Mary." But new information can be challenging, both to an individual and to an organization. Companies need to be fearless about finding ways of learning and knowing that allow for deeper understanding of meaning, context and the shared experiences of everyone involved in their businesses. The key is to truly listen to the stories that customers and non-customers alike are telling about their lives, their cultures, and how they really feel about the company and its products. It is crucial to understand, on an intuitive level, what the community needs and wants.

Pursuing a bottom-up strategy means seeking enough inspiration and input to find the magic to drive innovation. It's hard work. It means breaking out of categories, words, and definitions. It means developing a renewed sense of wonder. It means really getting to know your customers, and suppliers, as people.

Here are some steps to follow in the pursuit of developing bottom-up strategic thinking:

STOP COUNTING

So much of modern marketing strategy takes the white tower, arm's length, and quantifiable approach to strategy. Strategy can't be so sanitized and kept so distant from what's actually happening in the market. Relying on quantitative models misses the point. As Friedrich Nietzsche said, "There are no facts, only interpretations." So many companies spend a great deal of time counting everything, but seeing the significance of nothing.

When you count things, you first have to define them in measurable ways, letting the system manipulate the figures by narrowing the definition. The reality is that the more you count, the less you understand. I often find that, when asked by a client to solve a particular problem, the solution becomes clear after spending time in the field listening to people who use the product. I *might* get the same result by looking at internal reports and Excel spreadsheets, but it would take a lot longer. I would also miss the opportunity to discover the unexpected, become exposed to new ideas, or learn how the customers' expectations of the product could lead to real innovation.

Meaning is best constructed as a story. As Joan Didion wrote, "We tell each other stories in order to live." Even numbers have to be integrated into a story in order to be made meaningful. Hence, to understand our customers, we have to seek out the stories they tell. It still comes down to using common sense and intuition. Strategy has to be based on leadership, enthusiasm, or personal engagement. There's no way around it.

DON'T BEGRUDGE COMPLEXITY

In its essence, truth is complex. You can't take the complexities and idiosyncrasies of the world and reduce them to black and white numbers and hope to gain any real understanding. I see this happening all the time in the sales department of many companies. Naturally, the focus of salespeople is to consistently hit their goals. In many instances, I've seen salespeople count orders that aren't really tied down or withhold excess orders until the next month, just to meet these rigid, predetermined goals. Instead of focusing on the needs of the customers, or even on the reality of what's sold and what isn't, the salespeople focus on the numbers that *supposedly* represent reality. Numbers can be manipulated; real people with complex wants and needs cannot.

The real problem is that quantitative tools for building strategy can't capture the complexity of human life. They provide a wonderful rear-view mirror view of the world but it's hard to drive a strategy into the future by looking backwards. Think about the stock market. We've become so enamored with the ups and downs of the markets that we tend to forget the complex reality of what they represent. The best market analysts are not the ones who can merely recite the percentages of growth or decline, but the ones who can use their intuition to correctly interpret the reasons behind these movements.

Even the way most companies view their own structure – as a pyramid – suggests a static, top-down entity. Companies must recognize the complex world in which we live and begin to see their involvement in it in a new way. Instead of looking at the corporate structure as a pyramid, consider seeing it as a living, growing tree, one with roots planted deeply in the reality of its environment; that has the sturdy support structure of a thick trunk; that has an efficient system to deliver the nutrients of the ground to the tips of the leaves and back again; and that has the ability to populate the ground (or market) with its products, its seeds. The only way to welcome the role of complexity in your strategy is to rely on more organic strategic methods.

BELONG TO YOUR COMMUNITY

So many companies have isolated themselves from their communities. It's easy to see what happens; it happened to me. I started Radar Communications, a marketing strategy and research firm, in my garage. While the garage was crowded, noisy and full of interruptions from neighborhood kids, it sure was fun. It also functioned pretty well. We were all generalists. There was no need for meetings. Everyone always knew what was going on. When we grew we moved to an office on two separate floors, and much more effort had to be made in order to communicate. Hence, there's less time for us to be out in the community with our customers. These days, it's also much more difficult to keep the internal community as close as it was when we started. It's not a bad thing. But it takes a lot more effort and management than it used to, and that all can get in the way of spending quality time with the right customers.

While growth certainly demands more organization, it also means that you have to make a greater effort to be a part of all of your communities. Many of our clients are big, complex business organizations and their executives often tell us that they're too busy to actually go out and spend time with their customers. The reality of doing all their internal tasks precludes the time or the energy it takes to get outside the confines of their offices.

In this dynamic environment, the companies who will be successful will know their customers as they know their friends. They will be creatively engaged in their communities. To be a part of these communities, companies must develop new ways to communicate. It is a prerequisite for social and emotional connections. They must form community network strategies to give them the ability to understand and react to changes occurring in every corner of their community.

ALWAYS ASK WHY

I was talking to a client recently about his company's access to customer information. He said that the company has spent the last decade developing enormous databases of information about their customers; they know precisely what is purchased, when, and where. But even with all of this information, the client's company was dismayed to realize they still didn't understand *why* their customers behave the way they do. All of the quantifiable data in the world won't help you understand a person's underlying reasons. It will not give you the cause, only the effect. Not only does the very act of asking yourself why force you to make leaps of faith and use your intuition, it also makes you more human, giving you the ability to connect to your customers on a deeper emotional level.

DEVELOP NARRATIVE THINKING

In this disruptive age, the power of stories is becoming recognized as an important tool. It's a move from cold hard facts to warm and fluid narratives. Patagonia has become much more than a company that supplies products to consumers. Through their narrative they've become a movement to save the earth. People crave a human connection with the companies whose products they buy. A cornerstone of branding is good storytelling – but it's a two-way street. Companies must learn to go beyond telling their *own* stories to listening to and understanding their customer's stories. By being more human and relying on storytelling and narrative strategic thinking, companies have the opportunity to be more relevant to other members of their community. Marketing strategy must be framed as a fluid, organic narrative instead of a static, immovable framework. It's the tree versus the pyramid. Telling and listening to human stories not only provides a context to people's lives, but also engages the imagination and interjects magic.

Founders of exceptional companies are seldom focused on their "brand" when they start their business. Instead, they focus on stories that eventually change the world, by using bottom-up strategy to see beyond the horizon. The reality is that in the start-up phase you inherently rely on your customers, suppliers, and employees to help develop your strategy. Established companies often forget this, and try to distance themselves from their turbulent, risky beginnings. But companies would benefit from rediscovering their roots and revisiting their own creative history.

THE ROAD MAP AHEAD

A bottom-up strategy provides companies with the flexibility to be extraordinary. They become more prominent participants in their own communities and have deeper relationships with other community members. The second part of this book is a map of how to become more actively engaged in your community. It's about taking a journey to create this deeper dialogue in the context of your current and future customers' lives. The goal is to provide you with real tools that have worked well in driving inspiration and innovation deep inside companies. Embracing a bottom-up strategy means becoming more sensitive to the subtleties of the environments in which we all live. This is easily accomplishable in seven steps:

- **Step One: Focus on Key Voices** – It's easy to get stuck in thinking that your customers see the same power of your brand as you do. You've got to get out and have the right conversation about your brand, with the right customers, in the real context of their lives. Every company has a small set of customers that have a disproportionately greater amount of power in the market conversation. You need to know who these customers are and ask them the *right* questions, which sometimes means the hardest ones.

- **Step Two: Get the Story** – The key in getting the stories from the street is to get deep enough into the lives of the people you want to reach so that you can understand the underlying assumptions of their lives. Only at this level can the useful context and meaning behind outward actions and behaviors be fully understood. It is the primary source for new ideas and product innovation. The only way to get to this level is by investing a lot of time and energy engaging in real, two-way conversations.

- **Step Three: Listen** – At the core of any relationship, a level of trust is required. People feel most comfortable with those who take the time to listen to them *in the context of their lives*. This makes them feel important, respected and empowered.

- **Step Four: Find Inspiration** – It's important to look in places in the market that are beyond your periphery but can bring unexpected insights and inspiration. It takes getting out in the marketplace, listening at the fringes, and understanding the power of community networks.

- **Step Five: Hone Your Intuition** – When you really get to know your customers who have the key voices, by using your intuition you enhance your ability to beat your competition with breakthrough innovations. Utilizing a bottom-up strategy gives you the confidence to trust your gut.

- **Step Six: Find the Center of Gravity** – All of the great inspiration that you gain from your customers isn't worth anything unless you can make meaning of that inspiration in the context of your company. At the core of finding the center of gravity is dialogue. This means that you have to maintain an ongoing dialogue among your internal team in regard to what you have learned from the conversations with your customers.

- **Step Seven: Tell the Story** – Products today have become less important than the stories they convey and the way those stories are interpreted by their audience or customers. Companies also need to have stories to tell internally – true stories that inspire action. They must themselves embody those stories with congruency and authenticity.

The rest of the book is a guide to bringing these seven steps alive in your company.

CHAPTER 2

Step One: Focus on Key Voices

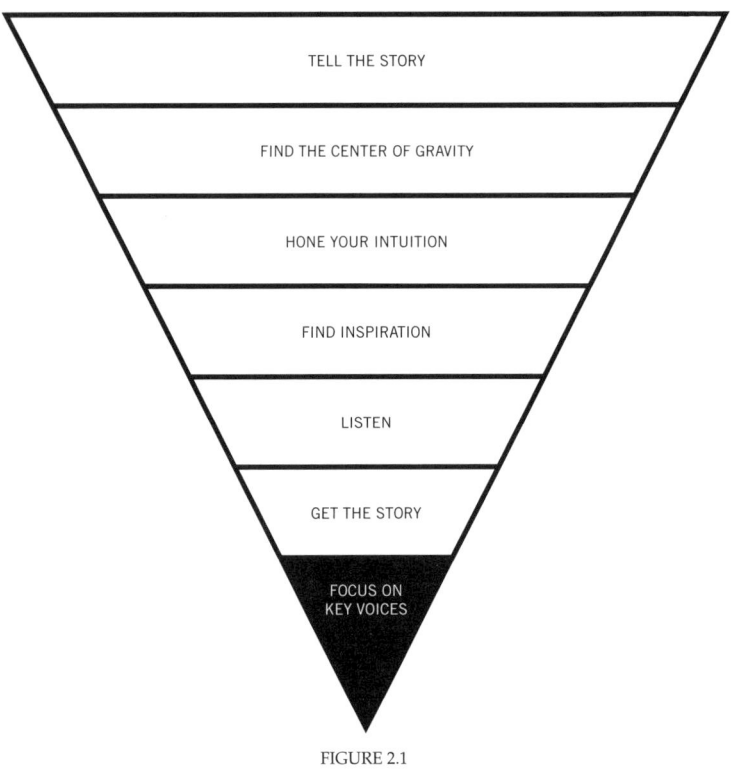

FIGURE 2.1

Successful companies understand the importance of identifying and listening to the key voices in their industries. People who have the key voices have been called connectors, salesman, mavens, deviants, and influencers in popular books and magazines. But one question still remains: How do you find these key voices? This process is much more than a business strategy; it is a matter of survival.

WHO DO YOU LISTEN TO?

In most industries, it is the opinion leaders or translators who have the key voices. Why? Think about an innovation in your industry. Has there been an innovation that started out small and then really took off? Think about Kodak. They *owned* photography. Digital photography went from something technophiles were into to the mainstream in the blink of an eye. This dramatic shift left traditional photography companies, including Kodak, Fujifilm, and Polaroid, scrambling to keep up. Like most revolutionary new products, digital cameras were expensive and slow when they were first introduced. After manufacturers focused on fixing those problems, digital camera sales dramatically increased, now outselling traditional-film cameras. Aggressive advertising by camera manufacturers did not bring about the shift from traditional to digital photography. Instead, it happened due to the adoption of the technology by these translators and their roles as evangelists to their family and friends. Digital photography's growth is now directly tied to its ease of use and quality of images. For a long time, film-based photographic companies believed that digital photography would take much longer to catch on because of the technical quality difference between film (approximately 18 megapixels) and digital (three to five megapixels) images at the time. The reality is that the average family snapshot needs far less than 18 megapixels, especially when sent as an email attachment. Another reason digital photography has spread so rapidly is that it has been so easy for opinion leaders to communicate.

Similar to digital photography, many other markets find that the real sales don't come until after the translators have been convinced of the need for the product. Once the opinion leaders accept a product, and the market is big enough, the product will spread like wildfire with little help from any formal branding. Opinion leaders help create an environment of acceptance and safety where more people can feel comfortable getting involved.

When I owned *Women's Sports & Fitness* magazine, we noticed in conversations with our readers that they often found themselves being asked about products by their peers. On average, each of our readers was asked for help buying a product by 12 of their peers per year. This finding became core to our advertising sales strategy. At the time our competitors had circulations of five or six times that of *Women's Sports & Fitness*. We grew our advertising substantially by helping our advertisers recognize that our readers were more important to reach than our competitors' readers. Our readers were extremely passionate and knowledgeable about sports in general, and they, in turn, influenced others. The reality was that our competitors' readers were seeking out *our* readers to help them make purchasing decisions. These other readers, who were not as passionate about sports, were listening to their more experienced peers. Our advertisers found that it was more important – and a hell of a lot cheaper – to engage in a dialogue with the readers of *Women's Sports & Fitness* than to advertise with our competitors. It seems so logical to skip the translators and focus on the middle of the diffusion curve, where most customers reside, but when you take a closer look, it doesn't work that way.

The reality is that if you don't connect with the trendsetters and translators, the rest of the market won't take you seriously. They will first look to their respected peers to validate a product they are interested in purchasing. Why is this? Well, most people that lie further to the right of the translators on the diffusion curve simply don't think about your product and the problems it might solve for them very often. Few people will be interested enough to do extensive research into the best products; most will rely on the recommendations from their peers.

So, what is a trend translator? In the last couple of years there have been several books that have described the importance of this group. Each book, from *The Tipping Point, The Influentials, Crossing the Chasm* to *The Deviants' Advantage,* has its own spin on what to call these early adopters. All of these books are based on the groundbreaking research of Everett Rodgers, who in 1962 wrote *Diffusions of Innovation*. In it, he outlines how different segments of a population accept an innovation in what he describes as a Diffusion Curve (see Fig. 2.2).

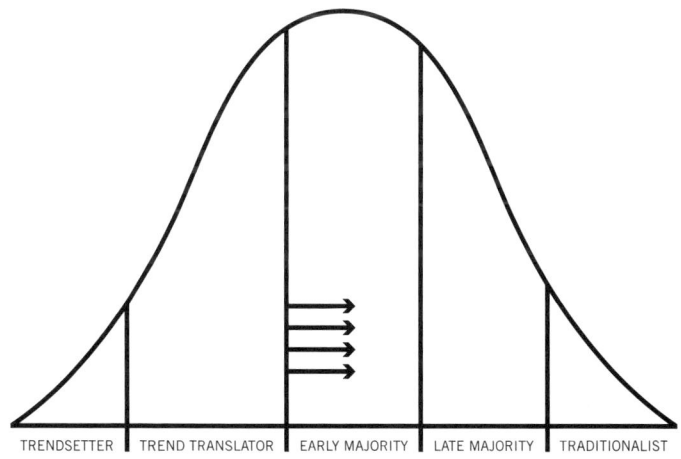

FIGURE 2.2 *The Diffusion Curve*

Rodgers observed that every population of potential users breaks into five categories: Innovators (Trendsetters), Early Adopters (Trend Translators), Early Majority, Late Majority, and Traditionalists. Each group differs in their value orientations. The categories are described as follows:

- **Trendsetters (Innovators)** – 2.5 percent of the population. Innovators are venturesome; they're always willing to try new ideas.

- **Trend Translators (Early Adopters)** – 13.5 percent of the population. Early adopters are opinion leaders in their community and adopt new ideas early but carefully.

- **Early Majority** – 34 percent of the population. Early majority members are deliberate; they adopt new ideas before the average person, although they are rarely leaders.

- **Late Majority** – 34 percent of the population. Late majority members are skeptical; they adopt an innovation only after the majority of other people have tried it.

- **Traditionalists** – 16 percent of the population. Traditionalists are tradition-bound; they're suspicious of change, mix with other tradition-bound people, and adopt innovations only after they become major, recognizable trends.

So, who are the trend translators? They aren't the first to jump on a trend, but they are inquisitive about ways to improve what they do. They are usually good communicators and are the people that others in the market tend to solicit advice from. Translators are individuals who achieve the capability of sharing a common language within a large group of peers, like our *Women's Sports & Fitness* readers. A result of this confidence is the ability to become a leader and a seer, one who is able to initiate a conversation about a subject they are passionate about, an idea or innovation they find of interest and value.

As translators, they are opinion leaders and always a little slower to actually make a decision about the acceptance of an idea or product than trendsetters because they want to make a good decision – good meaning right, efficient, etc. The diligence expressed by these individuals in their decision-making process is an important part of their psychological makeup. It is important to them that their peers see them as trustworthy and thoughtful, yet also progressive and forward thinking.

Despite the attention that the popular books mentioned above have brought to Rodgers' ideas, many companies have shied away from engaging translators in a conversation due to their relatively small numbers. Springing from the general corporate belief in the illusion of control, the idea of statistically verifiable sample sizes of customers is seen as a cornerstone of any conversation with consumers. The anthropologist Dr. A.K. Romney, however, has helped to overturn that assumption. Romney built a mathematical model, The Cultural Consensus Theory, which supports the notion that, when chosen well, small sample sizes of opinion leaders – as few as eight people – can be scientifically valid for conveying what the rest of the community thinks. Typically these opinion leaders in the social network can see further ahead, helping you become more predictive in your strategic thinking.

These translators are really trend *transformers*. Generally, they tend to be young, progressive, and artistic. They are expressive and thoughtful. When I mention the word "young," I do not mean in terms of age, but in terms of acceptance of change. Trend translators are always looking for ways to improve themselves or their experiences. They also tend to focus more on enhancing their experience than on being the first to accomplish something; the journey is as valuable as the final destination.

In some senses, magazines can be trend translators. They are trying to share an experience with their readers. However, their one problem is the lack of interactivity in a printed medium. The Internet, blogs, and social networks like Facebook and Twitter have succeeded in making the printed word more interactive. This interaction means that trends can flow at a much higher speed.

WHY TREND TRANSLATORS?

In today's brutally competitive business environment, it is essential to find a group of passionate customers that are willing to spread the word about your product or service. Without a deep connection with a core group of customers, it is virtually impossible to compete. Think about how this works among you and your peers. Do you have a few friends that seem to always be ahead of the curve?

I have seen it happen personally. I've owned a house in the tiny fishing village of Sayulita, Mexico, for eleven years now. When we first arrived in town, there was a tangible "buzz" that this cozy village by the sea was going to get very popular, sooner than later. It's a beautiful little town on an unoccupied, white sandy beach with a great surf break. When we bought our house, there were only a handful of *gringos* who owned property. Most of us were surfers who often let friends use our *casas*. Some of these guests went on to buy their own property. Then, our charming town garnered a full-page article in *The New York Times*, exposing the secret corner of paradise. The telephone at the real estate office in town started ringing off the hook. For better or worse, in the last couple of years the town has become *gringo*ized; property values have tripled, and there is a development frenzy happening.

The key is to know and differentiate your customers. Focus on finding the translators. Even if you want to get to know your loyal customers better, it's important to seek out the *right* loyal customers. Which loyal customers influence others? Not only does focusing on key voices save you money, it helps you understand where the rest of the market will be and gives you an opportunity to prepare for changes.

THE DOWNSIDE OF FOCUS GROUPS

Many companies still use focus groups as one method of listening to the key voices in their markets. While this seems appealing – and effective – on the surface, focus groups are harder than they look. It's easy to over-invest in pricey moderators and under-invest in doing the hard work of recruiting the right key voices. In reality, you've got to get out and really have a conversation about your brand in the context of your customers' lives – not in a pseudo-scientific setting.

In the United States, over a billion dollars is spent on focus groups every year. Focus groups are the current paradigm for most companies seeking customer input on new product development and marketing ideas; yet 80 percent of new products or services fail within six months, even when customer opinions were actively solicited. Likewise, most new television shows fail even after being screened by focus groups. Many people within the advertising and marketing industry question the value of the traditional focus group, yet they remain the standard research method, accentuating a huge gap between what customers say in the focus group setting and their actual behavior in the marketplace.

I've sat in an awful lot of focus group facilities watching people who are supposed to be customers, when it is obvious they are not. Before I started Radar Communications, I sat in on a focus group involving a new inline skate for recreational skaters. One of the primary screening criteria for participants was that they skated on a regular basis; it seemed highly unlikely the criteria had been met when one participant had to ask the moderator to identify the skate sitting on the table.

The reality is that, for many reasons, most focus group participants tend to misrepresent themselves or even lie outright. First, it's only human that when someone asks a question, especially in a place that is out of context, we all tend to guess the "right" answer. Product development and marketing shouldn't try to solicit one "right" answer from people. Companies need to hear what people really think about an idea, in the context of their lives. Isn't it much easier to be honest about any experience when you're actually involved in it, rather than sitting in front of a one-way mirror?

Another reason is that there is always some element of "groupthink" no matter how hard a moderator tries to stop it. There will always be leaders and followers in every group. There is one famous story about focus groups that has reached myth status. The story goes that an electronics company was conducting focus groups to understand customer preferences about a new portable boombox. Among other questions, participants were asked to pick between two colors: yellow and black. Everyone in the group talked about how cool the yellow was and that they would definitely purchase that color. As they left the session, each participant was instructed to stop by a room, one at a time. As part of their compensation for attending the focus group, they were being offered a boom box, and were able to choose between the black and yellow boom boxes. *Everyone* picked a black boom box to take home – the exact opposite of what they had said in the focus group.

Many focus group participants simply don't know what they want. New ideas are hard to articulate. That's because most of the thoughts and feelings that influence people's behavior are unconscious. There is no way to tap into a participant's unconscious thinking in the span of an hour, in an out-of-context room, with a bunch of unfamiliar people hanging on their every word.

Another significant issue is that many of the people sitting on the *other* side of the one-way mirror aren't always fully engaged. A while ago I received an e-mail from a focus group facility owner. He emphasized the implementation of an exciting new innovation for the industry… *exercise equipment in the client room*. The idea was that while the researchers conducted the focus group, their clients could be catching up on their treadmill workouts.

Focus groups, however, continue to be widely considered as highly efficient. The problem is companies simply hire a focus group company that can quickly recruit people off of their standard database and run several groups an evening in their facilities. There are many motivations for people to participate in focus groups, even about an undisclosed subject. Some participate because they need the cash; others come for the refreshments, or simply for the opportunity to interact with other humans. But are they going to represent the key voices you're looking for and give you honest, direct feedback and push your innovation forward?

In order for a focus group to be accurate and beneficial, companies must invest the time to research and recruit the right key voices in the first place. Finding and listening to the key voices of your customers takes a lot of work. You can't outsource every element of the process and expect to learn something that will inspire real innovation. You've got to get out from behind your desk – or in this case, the one-way mirror – and find ways to locate and really listen to those key voices.

FINDING THE KEY VOICES

One of the things we realized at Radar is that the current paradigm of recruiting off of an established list is antiquated, not to mention unreliable. Where is the value in talking with professional focus group respondents? Here are ten steps to ensure that you're finding, and keeping, your key voices:

- **Step One: Identify Cultural Cornerstones** – It's always easier to find the right people in the right places. Would you expect to find a fashion diva at a football game? Context is everything. Instead of just thinking about those people who you believe to be your brand's key voices, think about who they really are. Where do they hang out? What do they do? Are they online, in the mall, or hanging out at a friend's home? Get out of your office and spend time in your key customers' environments. By understanding the cultural cornerstones and understanding the context of people's lives, you can go a long way in finding and understanding them.

- **Step Two: Identify the Key Voices** – Once you understand your key customers' environment on a firsthand basis, start to look around and listen. Who is talking? What are they saying? We always ask people who influences *them* in their thoughts about a certain subject or product. By always asking people this question, you can quickly understand who the opinion leaders are.

- **Step Three: Make Them a Part of the Team** – If you want people to be honest with you, you have to be honest with them. One of the big problems with focus groups is that they are rarely honest – they exist apart from reality. How would you feel, and act, if someone was behind a one-way mirror in your office, watching your every move? In order to get people to open up you've got to get into their environment, be human, and do more than just let them talk. Let them lead.

- **Step Four: Create a Community Space** – When I was publishing special interest magazines, I realized that in order to be successful, it was my job to set a community table and invite all of the members of the community to it. At the time, this included employees, advertisers, readers, writers, and photographers. I figured if I was able to make one of our magazines a community space, where everyone in the community would actively participate in an ongoing dialogue, I'd be successful. In its essence, a special interest magazine doesn't attract everyone in the market. It *only* attracts trendsetters and translators. For instance, when I published *Inline Magazine*, the biggest magazine in the inline skating market, our circulation was 40,000. That's a drop in the bucket compared to the 30,000,000 active inline skaters at the time. Yet, creating a community space for this relatively small number of participants had a very large influence on the rest of the market. The community space not only provided a place for the company to connect with the key voices, but it also became a place for key voices to connect with each other.

- **Step Five: Create a Dialogue with Each Trend Translator** – If you really want to understand the subtleties of the marketplace, it is essential for each person you engage in dialogue to feel that they are important and honored as an individual. Today, having an individual conversation with each and every translator is much easier with the power of the Internet. Engage them in every corner of your business.

- **Step Six: Consistently Bring in New Blood** – Too many companies rely on the same key voices over and over to help them develop their strategic thinking. The reality is that any market is just too complicated to rely on any single perspective to understand it. When developing a dialogue with translators it is essential to refresh their numbers for every investigation. That's not to say that a few key voices shouldn't stay involved. But it is important to re-interview the translators that you are having a dialogue with for every project to keep things fresh.

- **Step Seven: Compensate Well** – Within the sporting goods industry, the common belief was that you could go out and talk to translators and pay them with a free pair of shoes – or better yet, socks. There was a feeling that people should be compensated for supplying companies with their opinions about product designs. But the bottom line is that everyone is busy, and everyone's time is valuable. Cash is still the best incentive, and I'm not talking about five bucks. For Radar's cultural encounters, spending time with reporters in their world, the average compensation is $100 per hour. That might seem like a lot to pay a soccer mom or a high school kid, but our clients are trying to make decisions worth millions; they need to hear the real story, and that costs money.

- **Step Eight: Respect Their Opinions and Time** – I've been in the field with way too many companies who consider their customers a necessary evil. It's always amazing to watch as a company has a conversation with its customers but doesn't respect their time or opinions. How many times have you heard someone say that their customers don't know what they want, or dismiss an idea as one that has already been tried? The superior attitude comes through loud and clear when you're listening to someone. Just remember, there is always something to learn.

- **Step Nine: Don't Burn Them Out** – It's easy to establish a dialogue with a key customer and then begin to rely on that one perspective. That person becomes your "go-to guy." It's great to have a few of these relationships in your quiver, but it's important to remember that while you might spend 80 percent of your life thinking about your work, chances are your customer probably doesn't. Connect with them often, but give them a break every once in awhile.

- **Step Ten: Keep Listening** – None of us can be reminded too many times to slow down and listen. You can get halfway to where you want to go if you aren't able to do anything else besides listen.

CHAPTER 3
Step Two: Get the Story

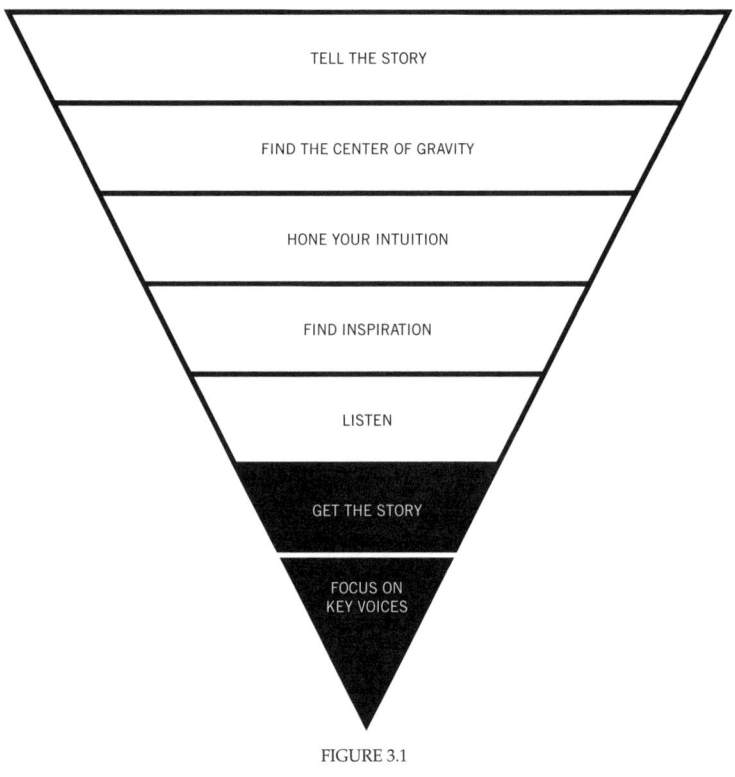

FIGURE 3.1

There is a story about coolhunting that has become an urban myth. Coolhunting, of course, has become a popular research methodology for companies, particularly when trying to make sense of the youth market. One sporting goods company is reported to have hired a well-known coolhunter to find the hottest trend for working out among teens. The coolhunters hit the streets of Los Angeles and started talking with teens, asking them who among their friends was cool. One name kept coming up; let's call her Rachel. The coolhunters approached Rachel and asked what "cool" things she was doing. Rachel wasn't entirely sure, however. She saw herself as a pretty normal girl. Then, after a few minutes of thought, she offered that, "I do jump on my parents' trampoline every once in a while…" That was it, the coolhunters decided: Trampolining is the next hot trend. Soon the coolhunters had convinced their client that trampolining was set to storm in the youth market. The client was advised to focus its energy on designing and developing trampolines and trampoline-based workouts for teens. Several months and millions of dollars later, the sporting goods company discovered that there was, in fact, no real business – teen or otherwise – in trampolining.

Coolhunting can be enlightening in a superficial way, but too often it doesn't go deep enough to understand the underlying assumptions of people's lives, behaviors, and actions. Such an understanding drives bottom-up strategic thinking. Only at this deep level can the useful context and meaning behind outward actions and behaviors be truly understood. It is also the primary source for new ideas and product innovation. The only way to get to this level is by investing a lot of time and energy engaging in real conversations. To participate in these, go to the source – out on the street – and get the story.

ECOTONE

Many models can be used to aid our thinking about the relationships that exist in any community or ecosystem, and how they might inform a bottom-up strategy and prompt real innovation. One such model is the ecological term "ecotone." An ecotone is a place where two different, distinctive ecosystems collide, such as where a forest and a wetland meet. In this zone, the ecosystem is neither a forest nor a wetland, but has all of the attributes of both. Ecotone is used to describe a place where evolution happens, where a natural dialogue is occurring. In the business world, all brands live in an ecosystem made up of many components. An ecotone from this perspective can represent the opportunity that lies within the overlap of a business or brand and its market (see Fig. 3.2).

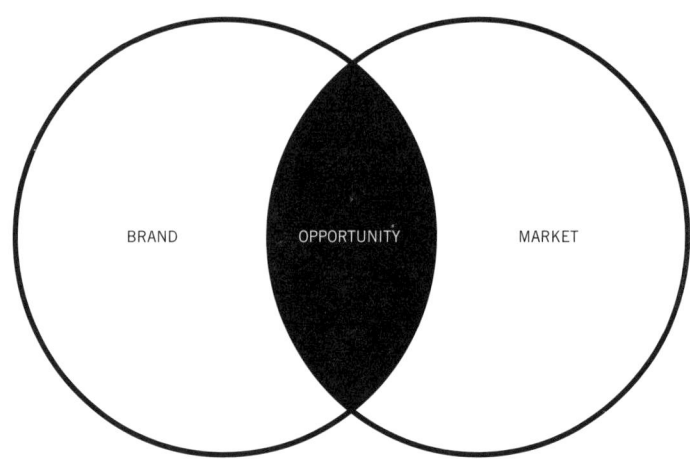

FIGURE 3.2 *The Opportunity Ecotone*

The bigger the ecotone – the more overlap between the two ecosystems internally and externally – the deeper the dialogue and the greater the opportunity for the business. For most companies, it is at the fringes of the organization that the ecotone exists and where all the growth in understanding and meaning happens. This is also true in natural systems, where an organism or ecosystem expands at its fringes. The key is to be sure that all of the growth that happens at the fringe, where customers are constantly interacting with your associates, is communicated throughout the whole organization. All too often, the learning that's taking place at the fringes never gets communicated to the core, where senior management makes the strategic decisions of an organization.

Many companies need help to guide the team that interacts with customers to tell their stories in a powerful way; this narrative is essential to presenting information that inspires senior managers to pursue new strategic directions. Only at the core of a company do changes in its soul or philosophy really happen. Chapter Eight will help you understand how to tell these powerful stories after they've been cultivated from the streets.

GET THE STORY

Before your storytelling can begin, you've got to lay the groundwork; you have to get the story. Developing a dynamic and integrative approach will provide valuable insights to your bottom-up strategy. We work and live in a very complex world. Try to understand and obtain information from the overwhelming number of relationships that we all participate in, both consciously and unconsciously. These relationships determine how a dialogue is conducted, and it is important to take some time to think about what each group brings to a dialogue.

In all of our businesses, we live in a complete ecosystem of all the participants and relationships that make up a community. This two-dimensional map is a place to start understanding the scope of an ecosystem and the interactions that take place as the foundation for a successful dialogue. This four-quadrant approach can be used to look at each of the ecosystems in which your business or brand exists. The upper quadrants represent individuals. The upper-left consists of I: you and your team and what you individually bring to relationships and interaction in the ecosystem. The upper-right quadrant consists of They: your customers or your potential customers, individually. The lower quadrants represent the communities that make up the ecosystem; the lower-left quadrant is We: your company or brand and other partners or suppliers that make up an internal team and have the goal of delivering a product to customers in the ecosystem. The lower-right quadrant is There: the outside culture where customers exist. This is the culture in a broad sense, including cultural issues, competitors, the political environment, etc. This map can also be looked at left to right, the left side representing internal participants and the right side representing external participants. When laying the groundwork for a successful dialogue it is important to think about the participants in all four quadrants and how they interact (see Fig. 3.3). An understanding of all of these relationships goes a long way in facilitating a deeper dialogue.

A BOTTOM-UP STRATEGY

The goal in an integrative approach is to find the ecotone, or center of gravity, where the participants from all quadrants exist in a place of common understanding. From this starting point, a journey through dialogue can expand the common ground and help to satisfy everyone's needs. Certainly, this is a moving target.

To explore and more deeply understand the intentions and needs of each participant in every quadrant, a good starting place is Abraham Maslow's hierarchy of needs. Many other models can later be substituted; using a few different models will deepen the understanding, and thus the quality, of the dialogue between each quadrant.

Many of us remember Maslow's model from college Sociology 101 classes (see Fig. 3.4 on page 56). Maslow, a humanistic psycholo-

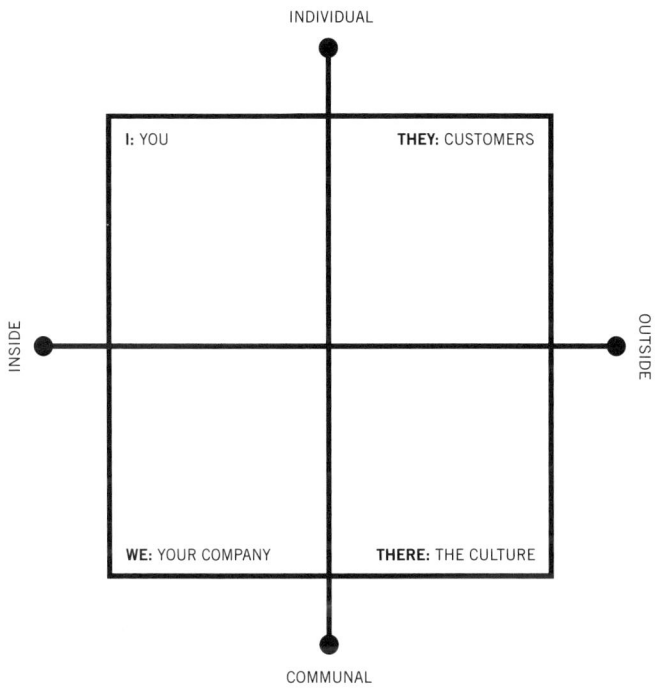

FIGURE 3.3 *The Ecosystem*

gist, developed a hierarchical theory of needs, often represented as a pyramid, in which the basic needs are at the bottom level, and the upper point concerned with man's or an organization's highest potential. Each level of the pyramid is dependent on the previous level. A person or organization does not exhibit the signs associated with the next need until the demands of the first have been satisfied. People, companies and cultures slide up and down the hierarchy as both internal and external factors change.

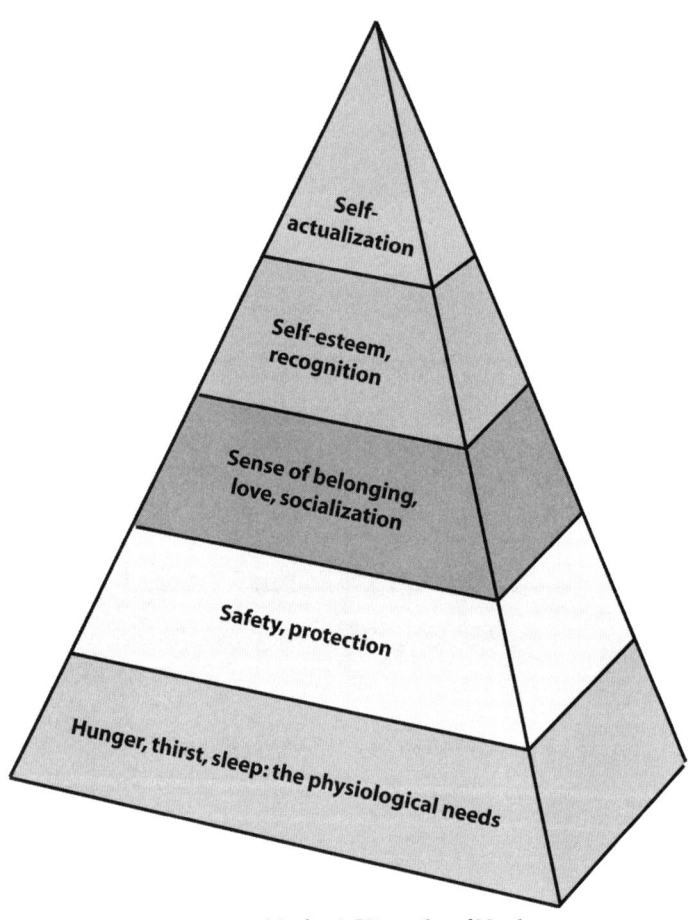

FIGURE 3.4 *Maslow's Hierarchy of Needs*

The different levels of needs are:

1. **Survival Needs**. These needs are the most basic and can be biological for a person or financial for a company. These needs are the strongest because if deprived, the person or company would perish.

2. **Security/Safety Needs**. These needs can be satisfied by stability in the overall ecosystem and become unstable in times of emergency or periods of disorganization in the social structure.
3. **Social Needs**. Both people and companies have the need to be liked and feel a sense of belonging.
4. **Ego/Esteem Needs**. People and companies need a stable, high level of self-respect and respect from others in order to feel satisfied, self confident and valuable. If these needs are not met, feelings of inferiority, weakness and helplessness can be exhibited.
5. **Self-actualization**. Self-actualizing people and companies are involved in a cause outside themselves. They are devoted and working toward something that is a calling or vocation to them. It is about more than money. It is about wanting rather than needing to do something. This stage is an ongoing process.

Historically, social sciences tried to embrace the more objective, "harder" paradigm of the natural sciences. As David Boyle says in his book, *Why Numbers Make Us Irrational*, "Numbers do a wonderful job of telling us an answer. But did we ask the right question?" Without asking the right questions, we will not get our answers, no matter how good the quantitative information is.

Qualitative tools for getting the story, such as focus groups, when used to better understand customers, have become more about prediction and justification (validating existing hypotheses, rubber stamping, and confirmatory) than discovery. Overall, this drive to quantify business in general has given us a much more sterile and generic world. It has made managers rely more heavily on numbers to justify their decisions instead of stories to illuminate their intuition. The context of the conversation and the lives of people have been stripped away from the process of finding the "right" answers. There are, however, ways to overcome some of some of these shortfalls.

INFORMATION SPECTRUM

At the ecotone, it is necessary to take information beyond knowledge and insight and move it into the realm of intuition, inspiration, and innovation. Intelligence to support a bottom-up strategy is usually done along a spectrum from discovery to justification (see Fig. 3.5).

RESEARCH SPECTRUM

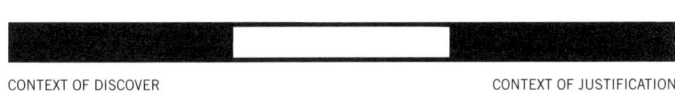

CONTEXT OF DISCOVER   CONTEXT OF JUSTIFICATION

FIGURE 3.5 *The Research Spectrum*

It's important to assess where intelligence is being gathered along this spectrum. If, for instance, you are trying to understand the future potential of a product, you need to use different tools than you would to test a couple of print ads. Unfortunately, focus groups have become the "one size fits all" solution for gathering intelligence for many companies. The important thing to remember is at which end of this spectrum you are operating. Too many times we've seen clients who want to justify something that they've already developed, when in fact what they are looking for is intelligence to discover the potential future of the product they've designed.

TOOLS FOR GETTING THE STORY

The tools we used at Radar for getting the story and in forming bottom-up strategies are taken from the world of investigative journalism and anthropology. They are simple tools that are often overlooked, yet they can help anyone locate the deeper human inspirations that drive new ideas. While there is no one right way, we like to use a dynamic and eclectic approach that we call "anthrojournalism." This term was first used in 1985 to describe the pursuit of journalism that went beyond the traditional journalistic questions of who, what, when, where, and why to examine issues. Anthrojournalism sees journalists and cultural anthropologists as workers in related fields, seeking different goals but sharing similar tools.

The focus of anthrojournalism is on the systemic nature of human relations and the cultural fabric in which these relations are imbedded. The goal is to find and report on commonalities in the human experience cross-culturally, giving participants in the process new and deeper insights that drive innovation and inspiration. Anthrojournalism can be defined as the combination of:

- Anthropology: A discipline that seeks holistic understanding of human experience past and present.

- Journalism: The style of writing characteristic of material in newspapers and magazines, consisting of direct presentation of facts or occurrences with little attempt at analysis or interpretation.

The aim of anthrojournalists is to develop deeper understandings of the communities they report about; they are willing and able to investigate and report on human events and issues in a comparative, holistic, and culturally sensitive manner. Anthrojournalism draws on anthropology's understanding of culture, and its personal, face-to-face approach to data through participant observation and ethnographic methods. It borrows journalism's communicative skills and its ability to synthesize information, its understanding of the cultural context of issues, and its methods of allowing events to be widely shared. The overall goal is to use a tool that seeks context and perspective in understanding human interactions – with not only each other but with their cultures, including the products that they use. In his book, *The Turning Point: Science, Society, and the Rising Culture* (1982), physical anthropologist Fritjof Capra suggests that "...in the future, journalists will change their thinking from fragmentary to holistic modes and develop a new professional ethic based on sociological and ecological awareness. Instead of concentrating on sensational presentations of aberrant, violent, and destructive happenings, reporters and editors will have to analyze the complex social and cultural patterns that form the context of such events, as well as reporting the quiet, constructive and integrative activities going on in our culture." Companies can learn to use these anthrojournalistic tools to help them gain a deeper perspective in the context of the community when gathering intelligence to inform a bottom-up strategy.

ANTHROJOURNALISTIC TOOLS

To better understand how to use anthrojournalistic tools, here are some principles to remember:

- **Be Aware of Context** – Unless you understand the context, you can't get the meaning.

    Only when a customer can trust you enough to be vulnerable will you learn their real needs and desires, giving you insight into the context of their lives.

- **Insist on Eyewitness Perspectives** – You have to be where it's happening, when it's happening. You have to observe and ask questions until you understand the meaning from the point of view of those involved.

    Only when you get out on the street and spend time with someone do you really get to know them. It begins with honoring people and spending time with them in the context of their lives, which then helps foster the intuition that drives innovation.

- **Holism** – Before focusing in on the details you need to look at the big picture – the whole experience within which a particular behavior makes sense. When you are developing your bottom-up strategy, you have to be able to think about the lives of your customers in whole, and not just from your perspective.

- **Dynamism** – You must seek to understand a living, evolving process – not a static snapshot. People do not lead simple lives. Likewise, their relationships with brands and products are dynamic, not static. Depending on who is asking the questions and what is being asked, the answers can vary widely. A bottom-up strategy understands the dynamism of the world and accepts the reality that there is more than one best way.

- **Descriptiveness** – God is in the details: the story and its meaning are embedded in the concrete, particular details of what people actually do and say. This is "ecological validity" – keeping the level of abstraction low enough to keep the story honest. Sometimes the story is obvious, but it must be described in the context of the organization listening in order to be understood. An honest description of the voice of the customer – or that voice itself – must be presented in the context of the company's culture.

- **Rigorous Subjectivity** – It's only human to have biases. Therefore, it's the responsibility of anthropologists and journalists to know their own biases well enough to be able to keep them from interfering with telling the story in a fair and accurate way.

    We all bring our own lens to the work. This lens includes our beliefs, expectations, values, history, and unwritten rules – as well as our ignorance, at times. It's impossible to get rid of our lens. What's more important is to recognize what we bring to the table and be able to put that aside and be as open and simple as possible.

- **Appropriate Interpretation** – While all human interactions involve interpretation, companies have become so sophisticated in their strategic research that they filter and interpret too much. The anthrojournalist's job is to give an audience enough direct inspiration to allow them to come to their own conclusions and point of view. Because of the context, the most important inspiration is ignored, simply because it comes out of the consumer's mouth first or because we've heard it before, telling each other, "They always say that." Many listeners are so educated and so busy looking for the golden nugget that lies at the center of an interaction with a customer that they lose sight of what's going on right in front of them – especially when sitting behind a one-way mirror in a focus group facility. As active listeners, people who are there to learn, it's important that clients not preoccupy themselves while an interaction is going on and then wait for the "experts" to offer their interpretation of how to divine inspiration, completely out of context from the customers.

GETTING THE STORY: THE RADAR FUNNEL

While there is no one right way to inform a bottom-up strategy, it's important to have a simple process that gets the story from the streets and is able to draw meaning from it in the context of the strategic question being asked. It is also important that the process have enough space so that one can be creative. In that spirit, here's how we approach the anthrojournalistic process to getting the story.

Using a simple process, such as the Radar Funnel (see Fig. 3.5), allows you to interject dynamism, which helps you to go beyond just looking and actually develop a new way of seeing. When you really are able to see something, you're able to see its potential, without limitations. By this, I mean the ability to understand the broader context of how strategic questions fit into a larger environment. If simply looking is to view things in the context of their limitations, then seeing is having the ability to see the limitations themselves, bringing a new awareness of the broader context of the world. In fact, most of the time the limits are ones that we have placed on a situation by the mere act of observing. When starting to use the Funnel, think about this difference between looking and seeing. Concentrate on seeing.

It's important to remember that you are entering a new culture to get the story, and the very process of entering into this culture

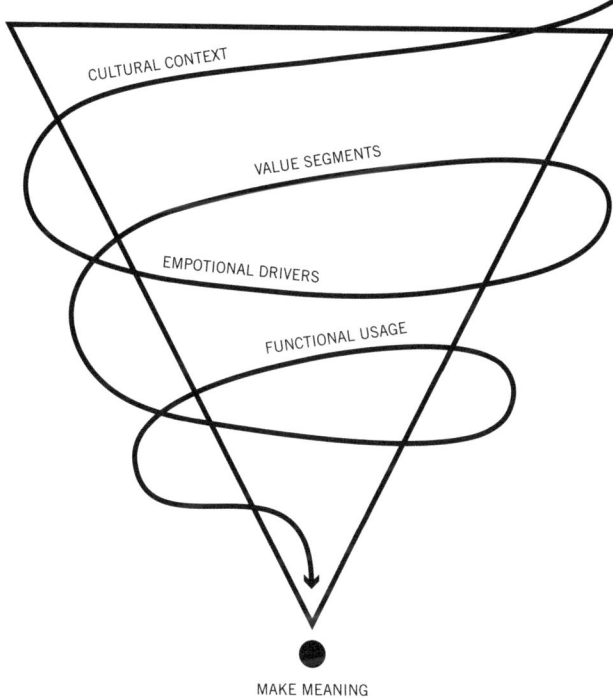

FIGURE 3.5 *The Radar Funnel*

alters the context you are trying to understand. Culture in itself is not anything a person does but rather what people do with each other, interacting as a group of people. As groups interact, culture is formed and transmitted through human communications. Remember that a listener and speaker have the ability to understand each other not because they have the same knowledge about a subject or because they have a common understanding, but because they both know how to have a conversation. Starting the journey through the Radar Funnel starts with a conversation.

The anthrojournalistic process should be viewed as a funnel. This process gives you the ability to ensure that the conversations you are having in the community follow a system and fit into a structure that leads to finding the center of gravity. The steps of the process include:

- **Step One: Recognize Cultural Context** – Many people who are trying to understand a culture start way too far down the funnel. They want to immediately jump down into the functional usage and explore the way their product or marketing is being perceived. It's great to be excited about going out and getting the story, but if you move too fast to understand the cultural context, things can go wrong very quickly. I experienced such an example just the other day. I was getting out of the water after my morning surf session in Sayulita with a friend who had been in the film industry for a long time. It was still early and the light was beautiful. We looked around and saw a photo shoot in progress. It seemed intriguing that such a thing was happening in our small fishing village. There was a large group of folks including a couple of photographers, a make-up artist, an art director, the director, some assistants, and several models. As we walked over and inquired what the photo shoot was for, a tattooed woman looked at us with disdain and said it was for the Buckle, a teen retailer in the U.S. For an instant, it felt like we were in L.A. It was obvious that Buckle's creative team decided to be sure their photos were authentic – so they jetted the team off to Mexico to enjoy a little of this authenticity. As we watched, the photographer directed a male model jumping around with a surfboard in his hand. The photographer was yelling out "Rub the surfboard! Rub the surfboard!" During the action, my buddy said, "Watch this." He quickly strolled over right behind the producer and said very quietly, "The surfboard's upside down." All of a sudden the producer started yelling, "Stop! Stop! The surfboard is upside down!" which sent everyone scrambling.

The creative team for Buckle thought that they could prove an understanding of the culture by spending a ton of money on a Mexican surf experience. The problem wasn't authenticity; it was that the team didn't know anything about surfing. Obviously they thought surfing was cool, so it became the theme for this year's catalog. But they could have been way more authentic by really understanding the cultural context of surfing, driving to one of the amazing beaches in Southern California and hiring real surfers as models. They would have saved Buckle a lot of money in the process – but missed a nice Mexican vacation on the client's dime.

- **Step Two: Discover Value Segments** – Once you understand the context of the lives of the people who are helping you get the story, the next step is to go deeper to understand what they value. Is it true companionship? Independence? Belonging? It's at the level of people's values and attitudes where the most inspiring stories can be found. You've got to dig deeply. Take nothing at face value.

- **Step Three: Uncover Emotional Drivers** – Once you understand a person's values, it's time to explore the emotional drivers that make them choose to take action. What emotional factors make someone want to buy a certain type of car? For instance, suppose you go out and ask young men about their relationship with their cars. They might talk about the independence that their cars give them. For most young men, a car is their first taste of freedom and the first environment that is theirs to do with what they want. While all of this is probably true, it is not the only way to look at these guys' relationships with their cars. How would your perspective change if you rode around with them for a couple of days? You might notice that when they get to a stoplight, and if there is a pretty woman in the car next to them, they might rev their engine or accelerate quickly once the light turns green. In this case, you might notice that one of their emotional drivers has nothing to do with the experience of freedom or the power of their own environment. Instead, it is all about showing off, power, and sex. Only by being in the environment can the emotional drivers be observed in action.

- **Step Four: Evaluate Functional Usage** – When people are trying to get a story, most of the time they start here. They want to show their customers a few samples or ideas that they might have, in an efficient manner – say a focus group – and move on. As we discussed earlier, if you are trying to conduct your investigation in the context of justification, rather than the context of exploration and developing your bottom-up strategy, then this is where you might start. There are lots of great ways to accomplish understanding functional usage. Probably the best is observational research. That means getting out in the field with a video camera and shooting lots of footage of people using your product. We've worked with a German research company that has a very sophisticated way of tracking where a driver is looking while he or she is driving. It was frightening watching some of the video, with a pointer indicating where the driver was looking. In one instance, a driver looked at the dashboard for over six seconds while speeding along the Autobahn. But what a great tool for thinking about how to design car interiors.

- **Step Five: Making Meaning** – Many companies outsource their conversations with their customers to agencies. In several cases, the agencies are also in charge of extracting meaning from the work they have just completed. While it seems efficient to let the "experts" make meaning, there is no way for them to understand your company's needs like you do. The stories that you discover must always stay in the context of your company and its heritage. If you are a clothing manufacturer and the story tells you to get into something far flung, such as cars, you probably need to dig a little deeper. Once you understand the story in a deeper way, what does that mean to your company and brand? How does it inspire an answer to a strategic question?

There is one important caveat to keep in mind when using these types of tools: There is simply no substitute for spending time with your customers, getting their story. There is no shortcut. Once you begin this journey of listening more deeply, however, a strengthened intuition can serve to greatly enhance efficiency.

CHAPTER 4
Step Three: Listen

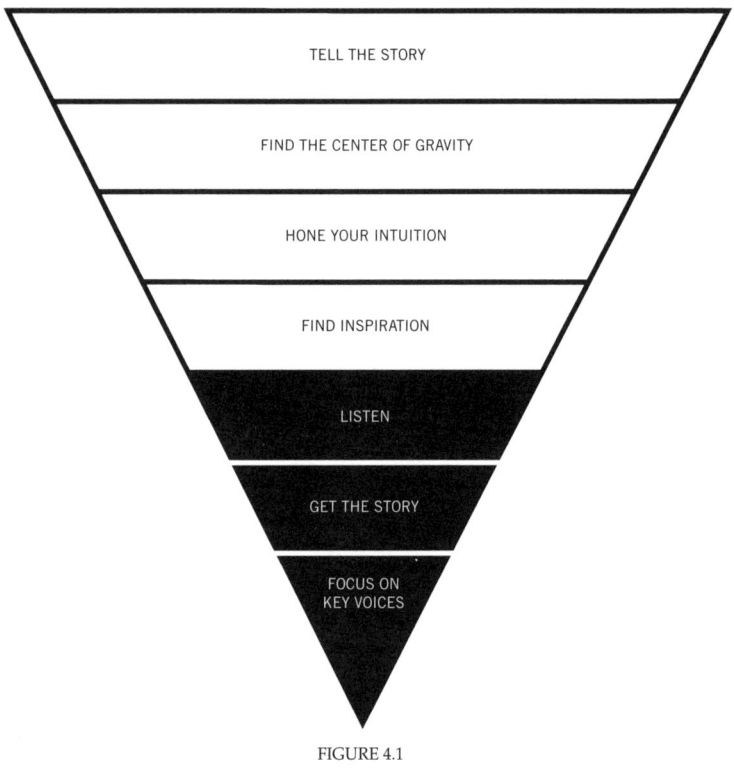

FIGURE 4.1

When I bought *Women's Sports and Fitness* magazine in 1990, it was just emerging from bankruptcy and teetering on the edge of existence. We knew we had to do some serious triage. I opted to follow the typical market research path: I hired a research firm and started running focus groups. After a couple of focus groups, I was horrified. These were definitely not our readers. Most were professional focus group participants who had been recruited from a database that the marketing research firm used on a regular basis. I was also shocked by the pseudo-scientific process of sitting behind a one-way mirror, examining the participants as I might in a clinical psychology experiment.

We immediately stopped doing focus groups and launched our own organic version of market research, hitting the streets and really listening to our readers face to face. We went to the sports events our readers were actively participating in; we found ways to spend real time with them in their worlds, within the context of their lives. By listening to the words and inspirations of our readers, we realized that what they really wanted was a magazine that spoke to their needs as athletes.

Following this deeper connection with our readers, we repositioned *Women's Sports and Fitness*, cutting the circulation in half to focus on the core of the market and changing the voice to represent the authenticity our readers spoke about. Over an eight-year period, the magazine went from the brink of bankruptcy, with a loss of 30 percent of its revenues, to becoming the leading voice for athletic women in the U.S. and growing revenues 300 percent. Its new position in the marketplace allowed us to broker a profitable sale of the magazine to Conde Nast in 1998. The innovative process we followed in nurturing the magazine was driven initially by the insight gained through conversations with our readers and observing their interactions with each other.

We discovered that at the core of the relationship with our readers there was a required level of trust. Trust is necessary in any relationship, be it one between a mother and her child, two friends, a boss and an employee, or a brand and its customer. Think about your own relationships. Don't you feel most comfortable with those who take the time to really listen to you? When you feel like someone is really listening, you feel important and empowered. Trust is a product of active listening.

Those same dynamics are very much in play for companies and their customers. Think about a product that you enjoy using and the company that produces it. It's great, isn't it? You want to come back.

Now think about a product that you've felt could be a little better, yet when you asked the company for help, they were unresponsive. This always happens to me with shoes. When I have a problem with something, like a seam blowing out, I call the company and can't get through to anyone. Nobody wants to listen. When I eventually do get someone on the line, I'm made to feel like it's my fault the seam ripped. No matter how much I might have liked that pair of shoes, I'd do anything to find a comparable pair from a company who appreciates my business and wants to listen to my problems.

In one of my business school classes, a professor shared an interesting statistic that has always stuck in my mind and continues to be a big motivator for me. He said that when someone has a good experience with a product, they will tell thirty people, on average; when they have a bad experience, they will tell approximately 300 people. Part of having a good experience is feeling that you're being listened to. Many times, even when a customer is initially unsatisfied with a product or service, they can walk away from the situation a satisfied customer – but only if they feel that someone has actively listened to them.

When you really listen, good things happen. Could it be that the traditional innovation process is getting in the way of listening to your customers? It's all about listening in your customers' native environment.

START BY LISTENING

Listening is a very difficult skill to learn. Asking a provocative question is one thing; listening well to the answer is quite another. Really listening depends in part on making yourself innocent again. Within any company, learning from what you are listening to means divesting yourself of all the baggage a brand has acquired over the years. It's so easy to hear something a customer says and quickly respond, "We've heard that before" without really listening to what that particular person is trying to tell you.

Listening does seem incredibly basic. Yet the reality is that all of us are often distracted and don't bring all of our skills or faculties to a listening situation. Have you ever left a meeting and wondered, "What did they just say?" When you are out listening to your customers, the first thing to remember is to clear your mind and enjoy the very human process of listening. This is a difficult thing for most of us to do. The overall goal of listening is to see patterns where others see chaos, and to make meaning that is well grounded in both experience and intuition. To achieve this goal, you have to capture the *vox populi*, a Latin phrase meaning the voice of the people. Here are some things to remember:

- **Concentrate** – It is very difficult for companies to concentrate. There are spreadsheets to fill out, sales to be made, and the bottom line to look after. How can anybody take the time to concentrate on listening with so much to do? Yet concentration is absolutely essential to effective listening.

- **Be Free from Anxiety** – This is possibly the hardest thing for a company to do. As a businessperson you know how hard it is to not focus, always, on the bottom line. It's hard to not be anxious about getting a product or service to market. Likewise, it is also hard not to think about accomplishing specific goals when you are talking to a customer. However, this is the only way to have a successful dialogue in which you are able to hear clearly.

- **Imagine** – Aren't all great companies started by someone with an amazing imagination? Look at Apple: it was Steven Jobs and his imagination that created the personal computer that fueled a revolution. Likewise, Nike's Phil Knight spent his first few years selling shoes out of the back of a station wagon. They were both out there with their customers, listening and learning. They were imagining ways to solve problems, whether for computer users or runners. Every great company has a heritage of myth and imagination surrounding its start.

- **Empathize** – At the foundation of most great companies is a group of people that embodies the passion and commitment of their customers and has a vested interest in doing things right. In essence, empathy can be defined as the ability to relate to customers in an intuitive manner. The most straightforward way to attain empathy is to be a passionate user of your company's products.

- **Understand** – Understanding is not about simply downloading a bunch of numbers and statistics and then analyzing them from behind a desk. In this context, it means feeling an impact in the heart and soul. It is an understanding that comes from experiencing what's really happening.

- **Love** – While many businesspeople might laugh, this is the start of great listening. Great companies don't just like their customers – they love their customers, and their employees, too. Look again at Nike and Apple. Both companies are on crusades with their customers to change the world. And their customers can feel the love. They recognize that these companies really care about them and want to spend time with them. It's all about letting people talk and tell their stories without any screens or interruptions. It's about slowing down enough to have the time to engage people in a passionate dialogue while in the context of their lives.

USE MORE THAN YOUR EARS

Scientists suggest that 70 percent of human communication is non-verbal. If that's true, then it is especially important to learn to listen with your eyes. The idea of visual listening is critical to the success of understanding what the market is saying through the stories they tell. Just as there is body language, there is market language. To hear and understand this language, it is essential that not only your eyes but all of your personal senses – and your company's senses – be engaged, to really understand what is happening. Shunryu Suzuki called this ability to look at the world with fresh eyes and an open spirit the "beginner's mind." When you have the open spirit of a beginner's mind you are more excited to participate creatively in the learning process as a journey, allowing the exploration to take you where it is going.

Cultural anthropologists use the iceberg as a metaphor for the layers involved in getting to know someone. Above the water line, at the tip of the iceberg, are all of the observable artifacts of a person or culture. Just below the surface lies what a person says they value – the things that might be learned from a quick interview or survey. But the underlying assumptions of people's lives reside at a much greater depth. This is where the context and meaning behind outward actions and behaviors can be understood. It is also the primary source for new ideas and product innovation. The only way to get to this level is by investing real time and energy.

Listening needs to be a journey, not a destination. In order to really hear what is going on, you must be open to any experience that comes along on your journey and be ready to experience it with a beginner's mind. The first step on this journey is to recognize markets as dialogue.

UNDERSTANDING MARKETS AS DIALOGUE

Currently, most companies employ complicated metrics or very limited qualitative methodologies to do their listening. As the world becomes a more complicated place with more white noise, there is a real need for new, dynamic listening skills that go beyond the intention of slowing down and listening to the market. Many individuals inside companies have discovered this fact and have come up with their own organic, ad hoc methods of listening using tools such as Google and Twitter search. Regardless of how listening happens (once it's recognized that it needs to happen) and assuming that humanistic tools have been successfully applied to that listening, the bigger issue becomes having the structure to communicate your findings across the company: you have to focus on both getting and telling the story.

It is often very difficult for those at the core of a business, who are in charge of making strategic decisions, to hear for themselves what is happening with their customers. But these are the very people who need to listen to their customers most. If they can't (or won't) do so firsthand, then the information has to be carefully and accurately translated for them by other members of the team. If the team can successfully understand their markets as dialogue, then their participation in the collective conversation with customers will be more rewarding, and the results will be easier to understand and communicate throughout the company.

It's critical to recognize the importance of the relationship between you and your customers as people. Nathan Schwartz Salant develops this idea in his book, *The Mystery of Human Relationships*.

Salant proposes that what you know of another person is really not that person at all, but rather a third entity: the relationship itself. This idea comes from the world of psychotherapy, in which therapists are cautioned not to project their own biases onto a patient. Projecting biases while listening to feedback only muddies the waters. It is imperative that listening be done with an open mind, and that we both know and account for the particular lens through which we interpret reality. There is no way to completely remove our lens. However, it is essential that we know what we bring to any conversation.

WHAT ARE YOUR CUSTOMERS REALLY SAYING?

Real listening means doing so in a way that facilitates real understanding. Have you ever had "experts" talk about your customers in a way that just didn't seem connected? They might truly believe they're saying all the right things – what they want you to hear – but much information can become lost in their "expert" translation. When you start to eliminate the middlemen and do your own listening, you'll develop a sense of knowing in your gut whether the information you're getting is lacking something, out of touch, or just plain wrong.

The problem is not the industry experts themselves. Much can be learned from and gained by listening to people who know a lot about any given subject. But if we put too much emphasis on their individual opinions, perspectives, or views, we're simply giving them too much power. Remember the old saying, "Don't put all your eggs in one basket?" Don't be too quick to put all your trust in any one "expert."

Interpreting the marketplace could be compared to the neck of an hourglass – if the neck moves even slightly, the flow of the sand is dramatically altered. When anyone tries to interpret what's happening in the market, they often bring their own altering biases to the process and might only look at a static portion of the market to make their interpretation. Every company has to interpret or at least make some sense of the knowledge gained from the marketplace. It is not good to completely relinquish this important process to a third party. Assigning someone else the job of listening for your company is a lot like hiring a translator; you are not always told exactly what was said. Your translator is really telling you what he thought he understood to be said. You need to trust yourself, your team, and your company to do at least some of your own listening.

ESHO FUNI

In order to understand how to start a dialogue and where things should go next, it is good to understand what an ideal relationship is. Here's one way to think about it:

Esho funi is a central tenet in Japanese Buddhism. It means that a person is at one with his or her environment; where one actually becomes indistinguishable from his/her environment. Nichiren Daishonin, the 13th century Japanese sage, expressed it in one of his writings: "Environment is like the shadow – and life, the body. Without the body there can be no shadow. Similarly, without life, environment cannot exist, even though life is supported by its environment."

The principle of *esho funi* suggests that we are not simply conditioned by our environment, including our customers and the marketplace. We are actually compelled to live our best within it; because there is no essential difference between our lives and our environment, our lives actually affect our environment and vice-versa. Think of it this way: How do you feel when you walk into a favorite store? Do you feel like you've entered an environment synonymous with the store's focus? Can you and your company be at one with your customers and the marketplace? Can you be the center of your community?

We typically regard the environment and the individual as two separate phenomena; we even see ourselves as having an "inside" and "outside," with our skin as a kind of dividing line. But if we really think about it, we know that human existence is impossible to sustain without a supportive environment. An individual without food, water, and air from the environment will die. Similarly, human beings can either support and protect the environment, or damage and pollute it. So although we tend to see self and environment separately, in reality they are intimately connected.

We often blame people and situations "outside" our control for the circumstances we find ourselves in. But the principle of *esho funi* shows that because the individual and his environment are inseparable, both the causes and the solutions to our problems are not "outside" but, rather, lie within us. *Esho funi* teaches us that we don't have to wait for anyone or anything else to make change. It starts with us. Any change in the environment is a manifestation of a simultaneous change taking place within individuals.

HAVING A DIALOGUE WITH YOUR CUSTOMERS

Listening is the start of a dialogue, which is the basis, or beginning, of a relationship. If a relationship is what a company is trying to establish with people, then how do you create a dialogue? A dialogue is all about give and take. It is about active listening, not for the sake of getting your point across or waiting for your turn to speak, but for the sake of learning. Learning is all about destroying old concepts and preconceptions. For companies, learning is also about growing. It is about extending a philosophy that goes beyond the production paradigm. Just like individuals, brands that tend to only talk without listening or learning have a very difficult time growing. The act of offering silence is what makes your customer's voice powerful. As the apostle Paul said, faith comes from listening. Brands must have faith that their customer's voice is important and will help them succeed.

Listening by going native involves promoting an outside-in, or open, system. A closed system does not have the necessary semi-permeable boundaries for information to come in and go out. By definition, a closed system cannot be a learning system, and eventually will die from sucking its own exhaust. All new learning also involves disequilibrium, a letting go – perhaps an unlearning, or moving out of the status quo for a while – then finding new balance. As Kegan so elegantly explains in *The Evolving Self*, "Every new balance represents a capacity to listen to what I could only hear irritably, and a capacity to hear irritably what before I could not hear at all!" How could you ever learn anything if you spent all your time talking?

Going native is a journey with no starting point or end. In order to grow, it is essential to think about a brand as a set of experiences and relationships. Those experiences and relationships must supersede accomplishments. It's easy for brands to get stuck in the rut of relying on a historical path of accomplishments. Instead, there needs to be a constant balance between exploration and accomplishment, and that balance point will always be shifting. It will never be an either/or proposition. Both must happen, and can happen, but not if a company is unwilling to fail or to try anything new, for fear of not living up to past accomplishments. Great relationships often involve taking risks, going places that you've never gone before, trusting in the unknown and trusting in the relationship itself. When your company can look at itself and its brand this way, your journey will begin.

Most listening in an organization really happens at its extremities, where people inside the company actually interact on a daily basis with their customers. At the core of the company, the furthest away from such interactions, lies the heart of the strategic process. The greatest opportunities for learning and listening, then, are at the edges of the organization. Yet, social networks like Facebook and Twitter are making it possible for anyone to listen.

SYNCHRONICITY

One goal of active listening is to be in sync with your customers. In *The Natural History of the Senses*, author Diane Ackerman asks an interesting question: If a red apple falls from a tree and nobody sees it, is it still red? Ackerman's answer is no; the color red is dependent on the light that is reflected off of the apple and onto our own retina. But most other animals see the world in black and white. Likewise, most of us see the world with at least slightly different perspectives. Unfortunately, many companies have actually become divorced from the world around them. They don't have a shared perspective at all. They must find a way to reconnect with the world before they can hope to listen to their customers. The key to active listening is to first become in sync with their surroundings.

If synchronicity is the magic formula, then how do companies reconnect and become consistently synchronized with their customers and their environment? When humans enter REM sleep our bodies operate at a frequency of 8 to 13 hertz. The earth's natural rhythm is 10 hertz. We seek synchronicity, and organically, we find it.

Companies can achieve synchronicity by going beyond the old model – of us and them, producer and consumer, company and customer – and developing a more organic, albeit more complicated model of the relationships that people inside a company have with people outside the company. Concentrating on these relationships means thinking about the dynamics of any organic system of give and take, ebb and flow. A system based on a dialogue.

DUENDE

The poet Francis Lorca provides another perspective on synchronicity. In his book, *In Search of Duende*, Lorca describes *duende* as the place where a performer and an audience are in the same moment. Lorca talks about *duende* as being a deep connection and intense emotional involvement with music, song and dance.

"*Duende* is a power and not a behavior, it is a struggle and not a concept. I have heard an old master guitarist say, '*Duende* is not in the throat; duende surges up from the soles of the feet.' Which means it is not a matter of ability, but of real live form; of blood; of ancient culture; of creative action," Lorca said.

If you are passionate enough in what you do and remain open to feedback, your customers will sense it and be excited by it. They will realize at a deep level that they are witnessing more than just a showy display of branding; they are hearing an authentic voice based on a deeply rooted understanding that comes from listening and being a part of the culture. Even big businesses can attain this. Think about a company like Intel that has achieved such a position through their unwavering passion around computer chip design. Great branding is based on real understanding, which is gained from the insights and inspirations of existing in the context of your customers' lives.

Everything we're talking about here is based on trust. *Webster's Dictionary* defines trust as a firm reliance on the integrity, ability, or character of a person or thing. Nothing can undermine a relationship between a brand and its customers more quickly than a lack of trust. In any relationship, trust is the essential prerequisite for success.

Trust is not something that simply exists at the beginning of a relationship. It's certainly not something we can assume or take for granted. Developing trust is an active and dynamic part of developing synchronicity. Trust can only be built and sustained by keeping our promises and commitments – by having integrity. Deep trust can be developed that is also sophisticated and responsive. The key to creating such trust is listening, the willingness to be honest, and sometimes even bringing uncomfortable subjects into the open.

CHAPTER 5
Step Four: Find Inspiration

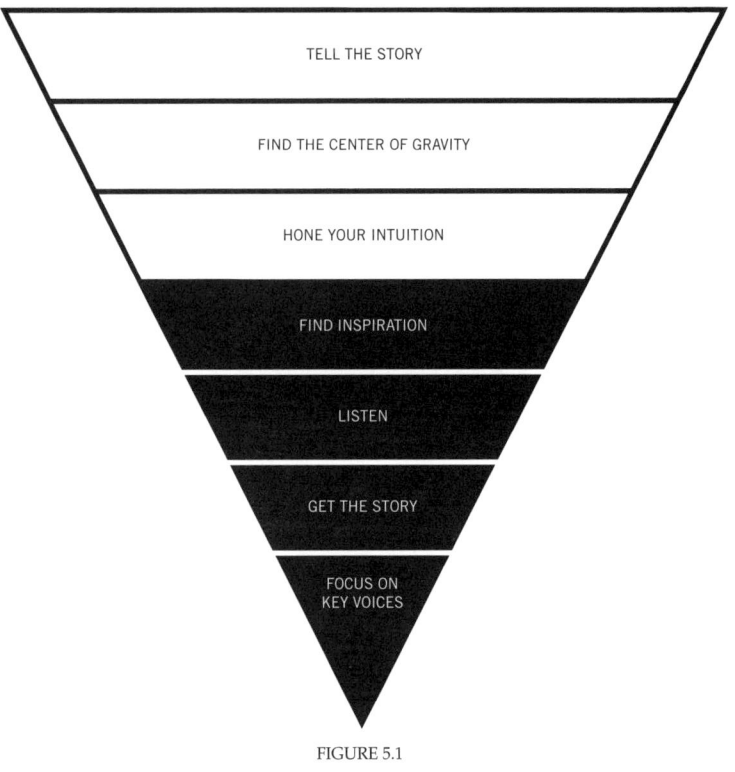

FIGURE 5.1

Sometimes looking in places that are well *beyond* your periphery can bring unexpected insights and inspiration.

LOOK TO YOUR PERIPHERY

Once you've identified the key voices to listen to in your marketplace, the next step is to find inspiration. Typically, inspiration comes not only from those key voices but also their friends and peers, social networks, and environments. We've all been on a treasure hunt for information at some point. We remember hearing something that could enhance a current project we're working on, but just cannot remember where we heard it. When this happens, you go on a treasure hunt. You think to yourself, "Who is most likely to have the information I need?" Obviously, you start with whomever you think will be the most likely source – or key voice. After interviewing them, you discover that they don't have what you want, but do know where you might go to find it. You've now entered your social network, and are beginning to explore the periphery of the network to find what you need. It always amazes me that after three or four of these conversations, I can always find what I'm looking for. Welcome to the world of networking.

SOCIAL NETWORKS

For good or ill, information about a company's product can be communicated in ways that will determine the fate of that company. To really understand what's going on, you have to go beyond the key voices you've identified and become a part of their network.

By understanding and utilizing social networks to identify valuable customers, you can get ahead of a trend and introduce a new level of strategic awareness that can drive profits in a profound way. Think of social networks as an early warning system and the key voices as your entry point.

Historically, social networks have been associated with the phrase "six degrees of separation," popularized by a 1990 play of that title and a later film, both written by John Guare. The idea is that that any human on earth is no further than six relationships away from any other person. Guare attributes this notion to Guglielmo Marconi, who supposedly said that wireless telegraphy would so contract the world that any two people could be linked by a chain of 5.83 intermediaries. Stanley Milgram put this "small-world hypothesis" to the test in a famous experiment in 1967. Packets addressed to a stockbroker in Boston were given to 300 volunteers in Nebraska and Kansas. Each volunteer was directed to pass the packet along to any personal acquaintance that might get it closer to its intended recipient. Instructions within the packet asked each person who received it to follow the same procedure. Surprisingly, 100 packages reached the stockbroker, each passing through the hands of an average of 5.5 people on their journey.

Many scientists considered Milgram's experiment ingenious, yet felt it did not firmly establish that everyone on the planet was within six steps of everyone else. First, 5.5 people was an average, not a maximum; the range was from three to ten people in Milgram's experiment. Second, two-thirds of the packets were never delivered at all. Finally, Nebraska and Kansas may seem like the ends of the earth from Massachusetts, but the world obviously has many areas that are considerably more remote.

A popular example of networks is the game called "Six Degrees of Kevin Bacon." This example can help show the way people are connected in a network. The game reached iconic status in a 2002 Visa advertisement featuring Kevin Bacon, with the premise that all actors in Hollywood have been in a film with someone else who is only six movie roles away from Kevin Bacon. Because popular movies are a small universe, the structure of this Hollywood network, with Bacon in the center, can be determined in greater detail. By using the Internet Movie Database, scientists have found a total of 355,848 actors, who have appeared in 170,479 films, all with some connection to Kevin Bacon.

There is even a website (theoracleofbacon.com) that keeps track of the Bacon network. This Hollywood network includes exactly one person with the number 0 – Kevin Bacon himself; there are 1,433 with Bacon number 1 (those who have acted with Bacon directly); another 96,828 have Bacon number 2 (those who have acted with someone who has acted with Bacon), and 208,692 have Bacon number 3. Scientists have found that because the number of actors is finite, the network around Bacon cannot continue expanding. At Bacon number 4 there are 46,019 actors, then 2,556 at distance 5, and 252 at Bacon number 6. Finally there are just 65 actors who require seven intermediaries to be connected to Kevin Bacon, and two exceptionally obscure individuals whose Bacon number is 8.

In 2002, Duncan J. Watts, author of the book *Six Degrees: The Science of a Connected Age*, replicated Milgram's "small world hypothesis" experiment using email. Researchers asked 61,168 participants to deliver messages to 18 targets ranging in location and occupation from a Norwegian veterinarian to a Siberian student. While only 324 chains were fully completed, those chains averaged five to seven steps, the same as Milgram's findings. Even though participation was low, the researchers suggested that college educated participants felt more confident they could reach their target and, hence, had a higher chance of doing so.

British psychologist Richard Wiseman decided to test the effects of confidence on networkers by targeting events planner Katie Smith. Ten packages (out of 100) reached Smith, in an average of just four steps. Wiseman found that senders who considered themselves lucky got packages to Smith more often. This finding supported Wiseman's belief that people who consider themselves lucky cultivate larger networks. These people expected success and were more motivated to continue the chain. Positive people who feel they are lucky can be a tremendous asset to you in finding inspiration in a network.

What does all this mean, and how can you use it? Well, it turns out that networks don't care whether they're made up of people, computers, companies or power lines, but they do exhibit similar behaviors. If all of these networks are also "small worlds," this has far-reaching practical consequences. For instance, a small-world Internet is efficient, but also vulnerable to hackers. And as we saw in the summer of 2003, a small-world electricity network delivers power well, but also enables minor faults to cascade into catastrophic blackouts, as happened in August across the northeastern United States. Networks can combine robustness with sometimes surprising fragility. For good or bad, networks exist. What's important is to understand them and be able to leverage their use to help inform your bottom-up strategy.

There are two things to take away from the study of networks. First, by using the key voices to start a process of social networking, you can better understand the social context of the inspiration that you are looking for. Second, by utilizing these social networks, you can find much more inspiration that can drive category-shifting innovation in both product design and marketing.

A great example of using the principles of networking is some recent work we did for Merrell. Once an old-school hiking boot company, Merrell has stepped into the core of the outdoor industry by developing a dynamic bottom-up strategy and tapping into the kind of network that can ensure they never lose the ability to hear their customers. You've probably seen Merrell's Jungle Moc. It's the comfortable slip-on shoe that nearly everyone wears, and many companies have copied. After Merrell introduced it, the Jungle Moc became a cultural phenomenon that literally doubled the size of Merrell's business. But unlike so many other companies who stumble onto some real innovation that resonates with the market, only to ride the trend into oblivion, Merrell wanted to find a way to continually fuel innovation. With Radar's help, Merrell set up a global network of people, all trend translators, who could consistently give them quick and vital feedback. To develop this network, we used networking principles to find the right key voices that could offer the best inspiration to Merrell.

The resulting network has been used for both tactical and strategic feedback. Merrell used the network to find global inspiration for innovative point-of-purchase displays, and also to understand how their entry into a totally new business category would be received. Most of the time companies receive this kind of feedback only after it's too late, when ideas have already been conceptualized, dollars have been spent, and egos are on the line. This all-too-typical path amounts to finding inspiration in the context of justification – and that just doesn't work.

With a preexisting network, on the other hand, Merrell can answer questions in the context of discovery well before anyone is committed to a specific idea, either financially or psychologically. This is precisely how Merrell has gone from being a small hiking boot company to a global force in both the fashion and outdoors industries, picking up *Footwear News'* 2001 Brand of the Year Award along the way.

Another easy and fruitful way to find inspiration by connecting with a network is to visit one of the many new websites that have built upon Milgram's "small world" hypothesis.

ENTREPRENEURS AND MANAGERS

Beyond looking to Facebook, MySpace, Twitter and other social networking websites to build your own network and facilitate inspiration in your business, it's important to find successful examples of people who consistently use networking for inspiration. A network gives you the ability to move incredibly quickly when using a bottom-up strategy to find inspiration. Such speed can give you an advantage in our dynamic world. One of the best networkers I've ever met is Tinker Hatfield, the design director at Nike. At the foundation of Hatfield's incredible ability to network is his natural curiosity to always look around the corner and explore the unknown. This is a characteristic of all creative entrepreneurs – being willing to take risks and possibly fail in the quest of acquiring valuable insight.

Curiosity is what makes most designers, like Hatfield, important in any business today. I've seen it play out in my own community of Boulder, Colorado, a small town of 100,000 people. Between 1998 and 2000, Boulder became one of the hubs of the dot-com Internet economy when six different companies raised over $600 million dollars in venture capital. Today, all of those companies have been shut down. One of the most fascinating things that happened in this mania is that people started to get confused about the role they should play in business; managers began to imagine themselves as creative entrepreneurs and entrepreneurs began to think of themselves as managers. This misunderstanding of roles added significantly to the destruction of these businesses.

A creative entrepreneur, or a group of them, traditionally starts companies. They are people who have a keen sense of intuition and can see beyond the horizon. Remember Apple and Steve Jobs – he invested the creativity and imagination that launched a personal computer revolution. Phil Knight at Nike spent his first few years selling shoes from the back of a station wagon. They shared their passions with their customers, and got out there to listen and learn from them. They solved problems collectively and created relevant products for computer users and runners. They were acting as creative entrepreneurs.

As companies grow, they need to have the controls in place to get the work done and actually deliver products to their customers, on time and at the right price. Usually, when an organization grows, the "creatives" begin to leave and the managers take over, although there are some notable exceptions (such as Steve Jobs at Apple). Typically, as the managers start to exert their control over a company, the imagination and mythology of the founder's creativity is squeezed out. Eventually, the managers become so busy working that they don't have time to connect into the networks that the creatives have built. It's essential to maintain a balance; to be able to listen to the network the creatives have established; to hear the inspiration.

What makes creatives so good at networking? One of the ways to divide the business world is into camps of static people and dynamic people. Most creatives are dynamic. Look around you. Isn't the world dynamic rather than static? Yet many business processes, as taught by business schools, are static. They try to take the dynamic world we live in and turn it into static data points in order to understand it. While that might work well in fields like finance and accounting, it's not a great way to find inspiration. Such a point of view proposes that there should always be a "best way" to do things – yet this is an increasingly irrelevant notion in a decentralized and dynamic world. In order to find inspiration, companies must embrace the fluidity of creativity and discovery. Finding inspiration in a dynamic world demands a dynamic mind-set for everyone in the company, managers and entrepreneurs alike.

Many businesses, inspired by their communities, have begun to install strategies based on design. Recently, there has been a democratization of design and an evolving expectation of aesthetic quality, but historically, function was everything; it was not that long ago that design was an afterthought. Amazingly, some companies still have this perspective. More companies, however, are responding to changes in the world that demand a new emphasis on the power of design and creative thinking. People assume a high level of functionality in everything from a disposable razor to a new car. The resulting plethora of highly functional, look-alike products in most markets means that the relevant, carefully designed products and messages – ones that find their inspiration in the context of people's lives – have a better chance to be successful.

Smart companies like Apple and Target have used a combination of design and network to drive inspiration in a deep way. Design and creativity have a new power in business that makes finding inspiration easier. This power can be seen everywhere you look: in fashion, furniture and household products. Design has taken on a life of its own, and has inspired a new level of consumerism. The reality of so many products being available today demands that design play a more significant role in the definition of each product. Look at many of the most popular products: computers, cell phones, personal organizers, digital cameras, designer pharmaceuticals, and information software such as iPhone applications. These complicated products have a real need to be designed in a humanistic way. A big part of making them successful is by using the power of design and the inspiration translated from the streets. The more contextual the design for the users of these products, the better chance they have of succeeding.

The power of design is as Marshall McLuhan saw it in the sixties: the medium is the message. The actual design of a product or message is what connects it to its user, and the design plays an equal role to the functionality of the product. Weaving function and form together is a much more difficult task than focusing only on function. Hence, finding inspiration that drives a design point of view is the only way to ensure differentiation in today's crowded marketplace. The key task in finding inspiration is to make it a strategic goal at the core of the way you do business. It's finding the philosophical balance between the infrastructure, systems, and bureaucracy needed to get things done and being flexible enough to listen to the key voices in your market and navigate their network in a way to find inspiration.

SIX STEPS TO FINDING INSPIRATION

The companies that thrive on and interpret inspiration into something real, have ingrained this approach into their company philosophy – it goes deeper than any individual. These companies all share some common attributes, based on good listening to their key voices and understanding how to leverage the networks that exist in their markets. Companies that strategically find inspiration time after time – from Apple to Nike – follow some of the same steps.

- **Step One: Stay Curious** – Have you ever spent time with someone who always knows what the next trend will be? The biggest factor is usually their sense of curiosity. Companies, as well as people, can be curious. The problem is that static systems stifle curiosity. Reintroduce curiosity into your company by changing the way you're looking at the world to a more dynamic perspective. Instead of focusing on controlling the outcome when developing new products and marketing ideas, focus on thinking in dynamic terms and accepting many possible outcomes. Such an outlook will go a long way in making your team more curious.

- **Step Two: Become Keenly Aware** – Part of finding inspiration is being keenly aware of subtle changes in your surroundings. Companies that are good at it spend a lot of time deep in their market's network. Only by getting out of the office and living within the network participants' worlds will you really be able to notice the subtle changes that magnify inspiration. Remember Jake Burton? What makes Burton Snowboards so dominant in their market is that they are intimate with every aspect of the marketplace, and know what network to tap into to find inspiration for new product and marketing efforts. As we discussed, at Burton it starts at the top, and that means that Jake is snowboarding 100 days a year. When your CEO is that well connected to the marketplace, keenly aware of the subtleties, and always knows where to find inspiration, it's hard for your competitors to keep up.

- **Step Three: Use Your Imagination** – I'm always amazed by the imaginations of my two little boys. They started talking around Halloween at ages of three. One of the first full sentences they both could say was, "Oh, no! Ghost coming! Scary!" and then they would run around the house laughing uncontrollably. One of the things that I am most struck by with small children around is that we, as adults, have lost our imaginations. The world is a serious place, whether it's business, world affairs, the economy or, for that matter, our entertainment. People took the Chicago Cubs' loss in the National League Championships in the fall of 2003 pretty seriously. Seriously enough to phone in anonymous death threats to the poor guy who made the Cubs' right fielder miss the foul ball catch. Likewise, companies can take things way too seriously. It seems that in today's business environment, recovering from a recession, there is a lot of underlying stress making everyone more serious. One of the key ingredients to finding inspiration is to have an active imagination. We all have imaginations but, like a muscle, you've got to use it or lose it. Turn on your imagination by doing creative things. Get your team together and have some fun. Do things that encourage people to find inspiration through the use of "out of the box" thinking. When you support this kind of thinking, new inspiration will really start to flow.

- **Step Four: Approach with a Human Touch** – I've been on explorations with clients where some team members are so focused on accomplishing the task at hand that they act more like robots than humans. When looking for inspiration, it's essential that you do so with a human touch. When you're out trying to explore newly formed network connections, you've first got to gain the trust of those in the network. If you're only there to complete your business task, it's obvious to others and doesn't engender trust at all. Being human means taking the time to really care about the people from whom you're trying to gain inspiration. That requires sharing a part of yourself. Being more human means being more vulnerable, and that's a very hard thing to do – especially in the context of business.

- **Step Five: Practice Patience** – The most important thing to remember about finding inspiration is that it's a journey with no beginning or end. Like anything else, most of us can't find real inspiration the first time we try. The first time you see someone you're not going to ask him or her to marry you, are you? Well, I guess it does happen… but that's pure chance. Finding true inspiration is something that you've got to spend every day doing, a little at a time. Probably the most important way to make finding inspiration happen is by integrating it into your daily schedule. Read magazines you don't usually read, go to new restaurants, stay in a different hotel each time you travel, and most importantly, talk to new people. It's one step at a time.

- **Step Six: Always Stay Connected** – Apple is firmly connected to the creative graphics community. Nike has a support system of athletes, and Patagonia is connected with outdoor adventurers. Who are you connected with? Are you networked intimately enough to your group of trend translators that you can call or email at any time to explore a couple of new ideas? Do you know them well enough that if they don't know where to find the inspiration you're looking for, they will turn you on to their network? Not only are Apple, Nike, and Patagonia connected, but they have become a vital part of their network's community, allowing them to consistently find inspiration for both products and marketing much faster than their competitors.

CHAPTER 6
Step Five: Hone Your Intuition

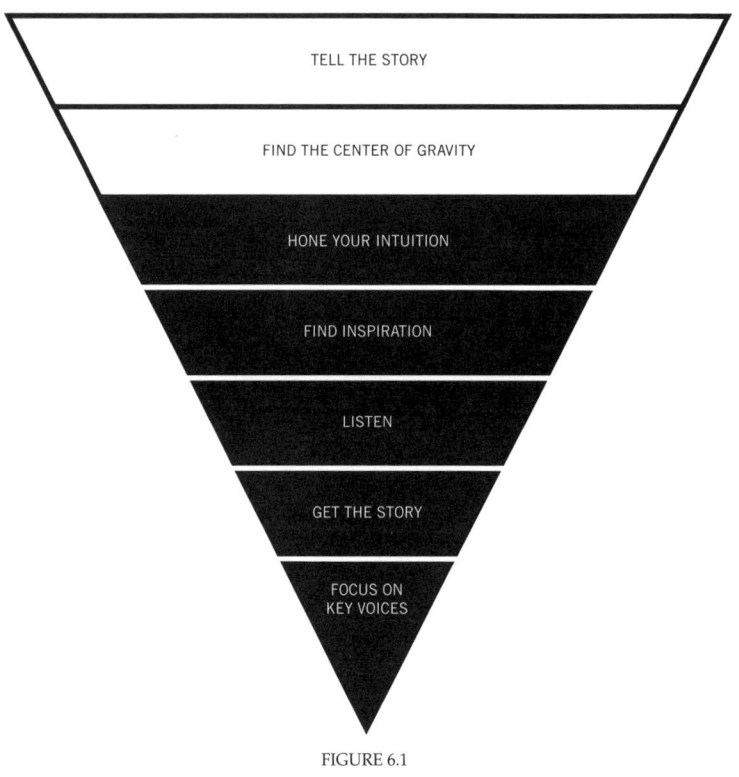

FIGURE 6.1

A few years ago Radar was working on a car project and needed to get a point of view before getting started. We hired reporter Nate Sherwood to talk to his friends about their cars and their lives, and recorded the conversations. What came back in a couple of weeks was a brilliant, inspirational video of Sherwood and his buddies hanging out in cars, drag racing, and jumping over cars on their skateboards. The videotape Sherwood delivered included clips from the video game "Gran Turismo" interspersed with footage about real cars. Sherwood and his buddies also produced a rap song called "Gran Turismo" to go with the video. When we later talked to Sherwood about his video, he explained to us that each of his friends owned two cars: the one that they actually drove, and the virtual car they drove on Gran Turismo. What stood out above all was the fact that Sherwood and his buddies thought of their real cars and their virtual cars with the same level of importance.

We were very excited about this reality-versus-virtuality inspiration and looked forward to sharing it with our client. But when we assembled the client's team in the conference room and played the tape, there was a general sense of disbelief. Of the 20 people present, only one person had ever heard of Gran Turismo, the number one-selling video game at the time. Nonetheless, the client soon came to embrace the opportunity that seemed to present itself – namely, to start testing the relevance of new car concepts in virtuality. The video game world would be a place where our client could have a deep enough dialogue to understand exactly what their current and potential customers really thought, in an uncluttered and cost-effective environment.

The dynamic environment in which your customers live demands that the tools your company needs to succeed must evolve. Today, risk-taking and creativity are rewarded more frequently; in many markets, innovation has become a winner-take-all game. In this kind of environment, you need to be able to reduce the time it takes to make good decisions. One way to do that is to increase the level of emotional intelligence or intuition. Intuitive brands show a superior ability to adapt to and capitalize on a rapidly changing and often unpredictable environment. Conversely, many aging companies have fallen on hard times because they have been unable to innovate and renew themselves. Renewal is an act of creativity. Something has to die – irrelevant products, brands or tools – in order for something else to thrive. Using your intuition can fuel this creativity and renewal.

WHAT IS INTUITION?

Most businesspeople are scared of the word intuition. They are usually not anxious to admit that they use their gut in many of their decisions – especially when those decisions have a good chance of being reviewed by their boss, their boss' boss, the board, or even the company's shareholders. No one wants to admit to a strategic choice "just felt right," admitting that they relied on something as unscientific as intuition in the shaping of important decisions. Some, in fact, are reluctant to admit it even to themselves. In the field of medicine, quantitative studies can tell you whether one illness is more serious than another, or that you have a 90 percent chance of recovering with no long-term side effects. But all a patient really wants to know is how to feel better. It usually takes a doctor with a highly developed sense of intuition to dispense comfort along with a cure.

Many people prefer the term "value judgment" when talking about intuition. Either way, not using your intuition – as the man found who drowned in a lake with an average depth of only six inches – can get you in trouble. Still, there is a reluctance by many, when exploring the market for innovation, to be more organic, to get out there and really understand the dynamism of a customer's world. It is said that after you've done something the exact same way for two years, you should look it over carefully. After five years, look at it with suspicion. After ten years, throw it out and start all over. It's certainly time to get out from behind the one-way mirror of the focus group room, get out on the street, and start using your intuition.

To be clear, let's define intuition further. By intuition I don't mean instinct, or primal drive. Instead, I mean intuition rooted in reality. It must be based in logic, knowledge, and most importantly, experience. Gary Klein, author of *Intuition at Work*, defines intuition as the way we translate our experience into action. You must be able to marry the rational with the emotional. Intuition has been called the nose of the mind, an especially powerful tool in developing innovation where there is little or no recorded experience to draw upon. There is a difference, however, between personal taste and true intuition. Personal taste can lead to disaster in the marketplace, while intuition can be the final touch in developing successful innovation. This very specific type of intuition is oriented directly to the market needs and is not geared toward choosing good employees, for example.

Intuition is a creative act that takes over at the edge of knowledge. It can assemble previously unrelated facts and experiences into a new judgment about an untried solution. It is also an individual process, as opposed to a committee act. As John Steinbeck said, intuition resides "in the lonely mind of a man." People who are intuitive always seem to have a healthy respect for facts, but they don't hold them sacred. They recognize that many times facts turn out to be little more than the judgment of another individual, or an idea that was incompletely researched or considered. Often you see scientific research later debunked due to a calculation error. Someone forgot to do the math properly.

People who know how to use intuition usually feel unshakable conviction and compulsion. We all know someone like that. A friend of mine, Ken Gart, is a master at retailing sporting goods. He participates in most of the sports for which he sells equipment, but the thing that separates him from the rest of the retailers in the business is that he also cares passionately about his customers. Recently, he gave me a tour of his new 25,000 square foot Bicycle Village store in Denver, Colorado. Just walking into the store, you could tell that it had something for everyone. What impressed me the most was that Gart intuitively knew how to organize this huge bike shop in a radically new way: He and his team had decided to arrange bikes by price point. Gart knows that the guy buying a $5,000 road bike wants to feel special, so Bicycle Village has a special pro section. Likewise, when a family is coming into the store to buy their kid's first bike, it's easy to locate the sign hanging from the ceiling displaying their price point. For most people, bike shops can be horribly confusing. First, most shops tend to hire ex-bike racers whose first priority is going riding with their buddies. Second, the bikes are usually arranged by brand, so that someone looking for a certain price-point bike has to go back and forth across the showroom floor to find the bike he or she wants. It can be an overwhelming and frustrating experience. Gart's simple idea of arranging bikes by price has resulted in a huge increase in sales, yet he didn't read it anywhere or hire a consultant to figure it out. Gart just knows what his customers need and want when shopping for bikes, and uses intuition to drive his decision-making.

Intuition is what really separates those who are good at innovating products and marketing from those who are great. It's the ability to weigh options and take a stand – even if the evidence points to a different solution. People who use intuition must also have the courage to put their reputation on the line in defense of their opinion.

Psychologists have recognized that intuition is a valid way of thinking, often producing better results than a more rigorously analytical approach might. The reality is that timing is many times the most critical element in the decision-making process. Also, in particularly high-stress situations, the typical business approach taken to solve a problem of evaluating options, collecting data and choosing an alternative doesn't work very well. That's not to say that intuition always works. But in a dynamic world, failure is an important part of learning. In fact, the reluctance to be intuitive and meet a risk head-on can often do more damage than the risk itself. This lack of courage can lead to a lack of confidence that will be noticed by everyone in the community. Such timidity is also a powerful obstacle to growth. It causes a progressive narrowing of the personality and prevents exploration and experimentation. The bottom line is that if you want to keep improving and learning, you must keep risking failure – all your life. There is a lesson to be learned from children, who are comparatively free from the fear of failure. Their questioning innocence can be of value in decision-making: They constantly experiment. They come up with unique responses and solutions to difficult problems. Yet many businesspeople, who are most in need of unorthodox approaches, often shy away from any ideas that challenge fact-based conclusions. They allow their fear of risk and failure to override the opportunity for potential success.

Like Ken Gart, the key lies in your ability to place yourself, intuitively, in the shoes of your customers and potential customers. In their place, would you buy the product? How much would you pay for it? How would you use it? The good intuitive brander is able to gauge market acceptance well because he knows how to identify himself mentally and emotionally with the customer. He can predict with some degree of accuracy how the customer will feel and react.

USING YOUR INTUITION

One of the most important factors in developing a bottom-up strategy is the ability to understand a large scope of information quickly. Our evolving world demands that we innovate more quickly, and that means using intuition. All of us have the ability to be more intuitive, but we all need to practice. One of my favorite sports – surfing – has taught me a lot about intuition. In surfing, everything is about timing. Unlike many other sports, the environment is dynamic. Instead of you moving through an environment, surfing is all about intuitively understanding the environment and being able to move with it, using the power of a wave to propel you. When you are first learning to surf, it's easy to be in the wrong place at the wrong time. Either you are too far out in the ocean to accelerate fast enough to catch the wave, or you find yourself too close to shore, with the waves crashing on top of you. When you finally find yourself in the right place at the right time, you are rewarded by riding along with the wave for a short while, getting an intuitive glimpse of its power and beauty. Surfing is especially hard to learn because every wave is different. The only way to become a surfer is to get out in the water and use your intuition to figure out where to be and when to be there. It is a lot like business. Intuition gives you the ability to consistently be in the right place at the right time in a dynamic world.

The only way you can learn to do this is to get out in the environment and practice. To start practicing, you must first forget what you've been taught about making decisions. Business schools have done a disservice to today's executives by downplaying the need for intuitive thinking and encouraging students to frame problems, formulate alternatives, collect data, and then evaluate the options.

You always hear the business myths about those who have used their intuition and grown grand businesses from those ideas: Bill Hewitt and David Packard in their garage starting HP, or Fred Smith getting a C on a college economics class paper describing his idea for an overnight delivery service (Smith later founded FedEx). Likewise, Starbucks' Howard Schultz found his inspiration while drinking coffee in a café in Milan, Italy; he knew a chain of such shops would work in the United States. Researchers are now recognizing that the most brilliant decisions are intuitive, driven by instinct rather than rational thinking. The idea that intuition is an important part of the decision-making process is not new, yet research from economics, neurology, and cognitive psychology is starting to make it a more respected component. What scientists have discovered is that intuition is a real form of knowledge. It may be irrational and hard to get in touch with, but it can process more information on a more sophisticated level than other types of thinking.

One of the foundations of economics is the idea that people make rational economic decisions. The use of intuition calls such a theory into question. Many behavioral economists believe that intuitive logic is hard-wired into us as humans; it is the product of millions of years of dealing with the demands of hunting and gathering. While computers excel at deductive and inductive calculations, humans excel at adductive thinking. Adduction is less like reasoning than inspired guesswork. To understand the differences, let's look at each.

Deductive thinking would suggest that all fish swim; this is a fish; therefore it swims. Inductive thinking: these animals are all fish; these animals all swim; therefore, all fish probably swim. Adductive thinking: all fish swim; this animal swims; therefore it is probably a fish. Adduction jumps to conclusions by connecting a known pattern – fish swim – and a specific situation – this animal that swims must be a fish. While computers excel at lightning-fast calculations, people are great at recognizing patterns. Psychologists believe that much of what we call instinct is simply pattern recognition taking place at a subconscious level.

Antonio Damasio, head of neurology at the University of Iowa's Carver College of Medicine, has done some very interesting work in pattern recognition. Damasio found that his subjects could recognize patterns physically much more quickly than they were able to verbalize them. He theorizes that emotions start the decision-making process, presenting the conscious, logical mind with possibilities. Without intuition, Damasio believes, the decision process would never start.

As suggested earlier, neither by-the-facts rationality nor pure intuition are right all the time. The best approach when trying to inform a bottom-up strategy is somewhere between these two extremes. The trick is to find out how much of each is needed. There are all types of problems, but they can be broken down into a few major categories to help you think about when and how to use intuition.

1. **Scarcity of Information** – It always seems that we have to make critical decisions to a new strategy without having all of the information we would like. When talking to customers, it often feels like it would be better to spend time with more of them and in different locations. When we are back in our office trying to construct the strategy, it's easy to feel like we've forgotten something. This is where finely tuned intuition comes into play.

2. **Complicated Environment** – In order to understand a complicated community you need to understand the quantifiable aspects of the market: How big is it? How many customers are there? Is there potential for an innovation? What innovations have been embraced? It's important to fully understand the how and what. Intuition plays a role here in defining the why.

3. **Short Timeline** – I don't know if this happens to you, but with every project we work on we could always use more time. In many cases, it feels like the strategy would be much better if only we could go back out and do more interviews, but the schedule won't permit it. The discipline of a timeline makes you work harder and rely much more heavily on intuitive leaps to inform and develop your strategy.

4. **Complex Environment** – This is an area where intuition takes on some quantifiable methods. There is just too much that is unknown. Most complex systems cannot be understood through a method of "take it apart, and see how it works" because the system is in flux and anything new, including your presence, changes it. In complex marketplaces it is important to intuitively look for patterns in the dynamic system.

5. **Chaotic Environment** – This is another situation where intuition can produce better results than rational analysis. Some parallels can be drawn from the chaos theory, which suggest that beyond a certain point, increased knowledge of complex systems does little to improve one's ability to extend the horizon of predictability. The only thing you can do in a chaotic marketplace is jump in, using your intuition to know where to start, and then try to make sense of the environment. This trial and error method is the most successful in today's typically chaotic marketplace, especially because customer relationships have become dramatically more complex. You just have to admit that you don't know the answer, and go with your intuition.

Using and relying on your intuition may feel uncomfortable at first. The fact is that no one likes uncertainty, and it's going to be hard to explain to your boss a hunch you can't really articulate, even to yourself. Even if you rely on quantitative data, it's important to recognize that it's much more subjective than you think. Remember, you had to choose how to define your study in the first place. Most of the time that's guided by your hunch, isn't it? Do you remember David Boyle's comment from Chapter 3? He says in his book, *Why Numbers Make Us Irrational*, "Numbers do a wonderful job of telling us an answer. But did we ask the right question?" You are already using your intuition every day – now slow down and trust it.

Gary Klein, one of the foremost authorities on intuition, only became interested in it after his research on the way firefighters made decisions wasn't yielding the results he expected. Klein's hypothesis was that when firefighters arrived at the scene of a fire, they would identify a couple of options and weigh them against each other. What he learned when he actually interviewed experienced firefighters was that they didn't really consider anything first – they just acted. They knew where to start, and would take that course of action until it didn't work and then move on to the next idea. They were using their intuition. Have you ever been with someone who's really good at exploring the market? They know how to find amazing inspiration – but they can never describe a logical process for it.

DEVELOP YOUR INTUITION

At a time when businesses are under increased pressure to be more creative, more quickly, in an uncertain environment, it is paramount to develop better intuition. Here are some things to think about:

1. **Practice Makes Perfect** – All of us have the ability to be intuitive; we just need more practice. Start integrating intuition into your decisions by asking yourself, "What if…?" Remember that intuition is a form of pattern recognition. It's a bit like playing chess. The more you practice, the more patterns you recognize. When you use intuition in a way that adds to your decision-making ability, think about what happened. Why did your intuition work so well? Did you recognize a pattern in your work and use adductive thinking to understand what to do next? Can you use it again in a similar way?

2. **Tell More Stories** – As we'll discuss in Chapter 8, when you are meeting with your team, instead of just presenting data or analysis, start putting the information into stories. Think more creatively; change the setting of the problem. Talk about it as if it were an article in a magazine: explore how the problem makes you feel and what your gut is telling you to do. Consider the possible endings of the article. Keep the stories short, so that others can share theirs as well.

3. **Encourage Others** – Using your intuition can be inspiring and contagious. Encourage others to flex their intuition by asking them to dig deeper into how they feel about information in a meeting. Remember that intuitive feelings are hard

to express and can be accompanied by a lack of confidence. Encourage others to verbalize their stories. Help make sure that intuitive thinking is supported but not over-analyzed. It's easy to get an intuitive spark, only to throw doubt on it by over thinking. Be positive and welcome out-of-the-box thinking.

4. **Listen to Intuition** – People can develop all kinds of reasons why they should ignore their intuition. Focus on what your gut is saying. It's not only listening to yourself, it's listening to the subtle signals in the market that highly intuitive people tend to recognize before others do. Also, listen to what your team members say about their own intuition. Ask them how a situation made them feel. Ask them to think about their feelings instead of the facts around a situation.

5. **Rely on Experience** – The best way to really grow your intuitive abilities is to get out and have more experiences in the market. Intuition is like a muscle; you can't sit at your desk pounding away on the keyboard and expect it to grow stronger. You've got to get out of your chair, immerse yourself into the market and start using your intuition. Start building mock scenarios around your experiences. Ask yourself the meaning of the things you experience. At first you'll make wild guesses, but after awhile, with more experience, you'll be more accurate.

6. **Integrate Intuition** – An interesting apparent dichotomy is that many of the companies that embrace and encourage intuition, are also very process-driven. Nike and Patagonia innovate constantly; yet have product development timelines and processes that are quite rigorous. By embracing intuition and creativity, and integrating intuitive decision-making as part of the process, the two seemly opposing forces enhance each other and add value.

CHAPTER 7
Step Six: Find the Center of Gravity

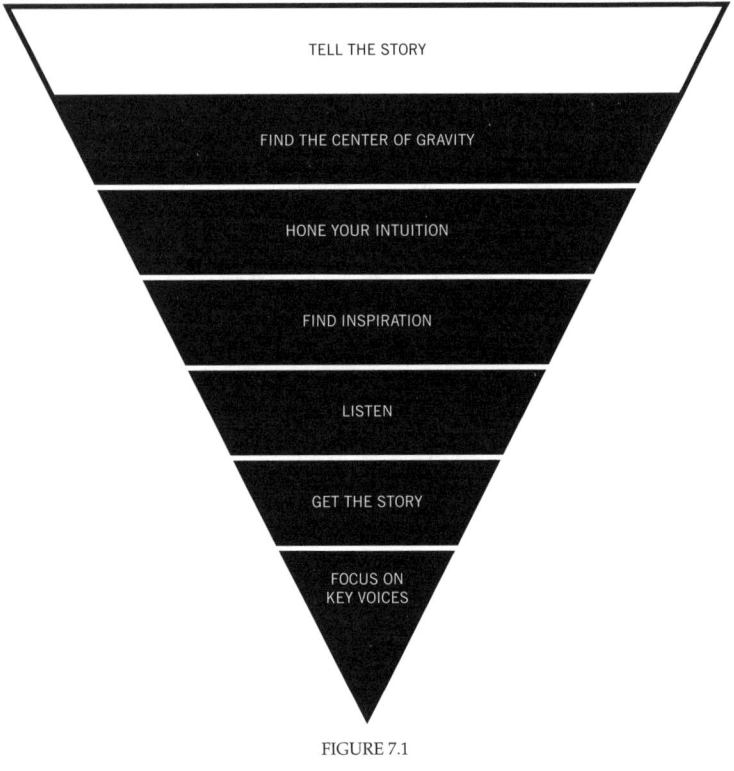

FIGURE 7.1

Radar was working with a technology client to develop new tools with the goal of enhancing their product design process. We had just finished a project focusing specifically on their marketing and were curious about how they integrated the voice of the customer into their design process. We asked if they had a bottom-up strategy in place. Our contact said no. In fact, he said, the company believed that their customers couldn't tell them what they wanted anyway, so why involve them? Instead, he told us, the company had a team of futurists that he called "the freaks," who sat around and dreamed up ideas. He continued by saying that they came up with some really crazy stuff, but that as a marketing guy he didn't get too involved with it, because it was rare that the ideas the freaks proposed ever reached the market. They were just too radical.

We think it's great that our client has a team of futurists looking around and actively trying to divine the future of technology and how their company can take advantage of various advances. But we would suggest that they may be better served by involving both the "freaks" and their customers, by stirring up all of the perspectives and trying to make meaning of it all. In order for innovation to truly move forward, a company must make meaning of all of the intelligence that it gathers. It must also do so in the context of who they are as a company. It is important that as you begin to make meaning you also find the center of gravity of the community, from which you can move forward – using all of the intelligence you gather from your bottom-up strategy – to better inform your innovation process.

There is an important dynamic between the left and right sides of a bottom-up strategy map (see Fig. 7.2). What we do on the outside (e.g. listen, collect stories, and have dialogues) must also happen inside, if anything is to come of the intelligence we gather. At the core of this dynamic is the highly interactive activity of listening. Intent listening is the first step in creating a deep dialogue and finding the center of gravity.

As I said, the goal of bottom-up strategy is to find the center of gravity, or sweet spot, where the participants from all quadrants of the map exist in a place of common understanding. When I was beginning to rock climb, finding and being fully aware of my center of gravity as I moved up a rock face was the hardest thing for me to learn.

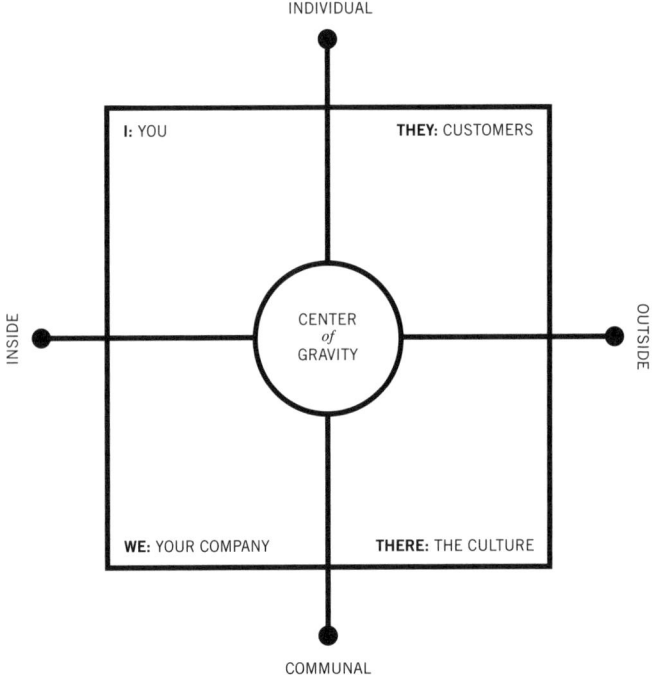

FIGURE 7.2 *Finding the Center of Gravity*

To climb well you have to climb from your core, or center of gravity. If you decide that you need to move your foot in an awkward way, stretched far to your side at the height of your shoulder, you cannot move any further up the rock until you are able to stand on that foot, moving your center of gravity over it. Rather than a physical place, when I climb, I've found that my center of gravity is more of a philosophical point. I can always find it when I feel in tune with my body and the rock wall that I am climbing. Likewise, when your company finds its center of gravity, it can move smoothly through the marketplace; it is in tune with its environment, or has accomplished *esho funi*, as discussed in Chapter 4. From this starting point of common understanding, a journey through dialogue can expand the common ground and help to develop a bottom-up strategy. Certainly, this is a moving target. A brand or company must frequently check assumptions and characteristics, through a continuing dialogue, to make meaning of and fully understand the center of gravity.

DIALOGUE

While many people look at discussion and dialogue as the same thing, they are not. Discussion leads people to hold separate points of view, while dialogue can lead to shared meaning. David Boehm, the British physicist, suggested a concept of dialogue as the glue that holds a community together. He describes the nature of dialogue by saying, "I give a meaning to the word dialogue different from what is commonly used. The derivations of the word suggest a deeper meaning. Dialogue comes from the Greek word *dialogos*. *Logos* means the word, or the meaning of the word. And *dia* means "through" – it doesn't mean "two. "A dialogue can be among any number of people. The picture or image this suggests is of a stream of meaning flowing among and between and through us. This will make possible a flow of meaning in the whole group, out of which will emerge some new understanding. This shared meaning is the glue or cement that holds people and societies together."

So, why is dialogue so important? Well, the reality of living in a dynamic environment involves greater complexity than living in a more stable world. Today, as evolution is happening so quickly in the marketplace, one of the issues that must be addressed is that the thought and energy to develop innovation has to be increased to understand the outcome of the innovation itself. Only through dialogue can you and your team start building plausible scenarios that can inform your search for the center of gravity and fuel future innovation. While some tools may help you guess the future, it is only through dialogue – in the context of a bottom-up strategy – that you will gain the ability to allow many different points of view to survive and instigate learning.

At the center of the dialogue process is listening. As Boehm said, "When you listen to somebody else, whether you like it or not, what they say becomes part of you." Listening is at the core of all human interaction. Through focused listening, in the context of a relationship, dialogue develops. Hence, dialogue cannot exist without both humanity and humility. Again, Boehm said, "An idea must be vulnerable – you have to be ready to drop it, just as the person who holds the idea must be vulnerable, I think. He should not identify with it. Dialogue, as the act of communally learning, can break down if those participating lack humility." This humility trait is sometimes hard to come by in business. Many people have been taught, especially in business school, the fine art of discussing and arguing in an effort to support their point of view. There needs to be a shift to an understanding that it's not about winning an argument – it's about learning what the market needs. Someone who cannot acknowledge himself as an equal of everyone on the team, no matter the title or experience, will have a hard time participating in a dialogue. Only when a person is ready to learn will he or she be able to participate in a dialogue. Alexander Freire said, "Faith in man[kind] is an *a priori* requirement for dialogue; the 'dialogical man' believes in other men even before he meets them face to face… Without this faith in man, dialogue is a farce which inevitably degenerates into paternalistic manipulation."

What are the skills necessary to use dialogue to find your center of gravity? To become skilled in fully participating in a dialogue, people must first discover what currently limits their own learning. Second, they must uncover the assumptions and beliefs that contribute to these behaviors. Once these behaviors are recognized, they must be evolved. These behaviors are usually recognizable by others: Depend on your teammates to help you discover your own limits to participating in a dialogue. Asking for feedback is also a great way to become more vulnerable and humble. The very act of asking for help can go a long way in helping develop a dialogue. Through this process, a new level of trust can be found, promoting deeper cooperation, which links to productivity. Through dialogue, you and your team can attain a higher level of concentration and efficiently reach your center of gravity, thereby making your innovation process much more productive. In turn, productivity creates more opportunities to have dialogues, and through these dialogues create shared meaning.

For any change to occur in a company, a team must have a shared framework and a common understanding of its center of gravity. Many companies are in such a rush, subject to "the tyranny of the urgent," that they cannot slow down in order to go faster. It is a commitment to understanding: Once people have really listened in the dynamic outside world, they need to spend time listening and in dialogues with each other to create a shared understanding, out of which aligned action and commitment grow. When companies start to truly listen and have a dialogue around the inspiration that they've discovered in the conversations with customers, there is an opportunity for real innovation. Customers can sense when a company is internally aligned around a central point of view. These companies tend to have brands that are much more intimate with their customers.

People are bound together not only by shared stories and information but also through shared understanding, or meaning making.

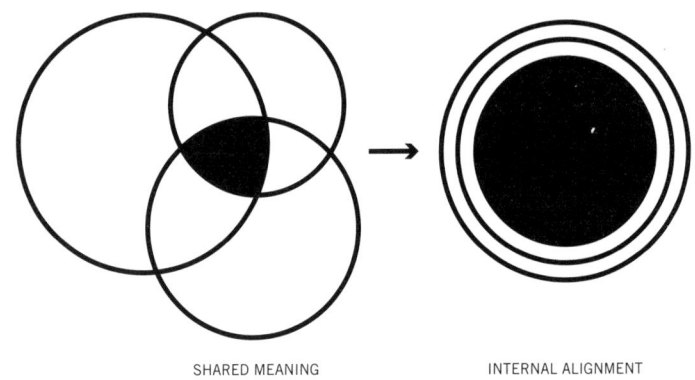

SHARED MEANING   INTERNAL ALIGNMENT

FIGURE 7.3 *Internal Alignment*

Once a team finds its center of gravity and a shared meaning, they can drive inspiration and innovation. When there is shared meaning about a problem or opportunity, there is internal alignment (see Fig. 7.3).

To find this shared meaning, storytelling is the key. It is the most ancient form of sharing information known to man. It carries our hopes, dreams and values. In the future, companies and individuals will find meaning and thrive on the basis of their stories and myths instead of data. The key will be to create products and services that evoke a deep emotion. Products will actually be as important as the stories they tell. True stories inspire action, and true branding is authentic storytelling. Listening, storytelling, and dialogue with your internal team connects you to humanity in the fullest sense – through intuition, creativity and innovation. By collecting the stories from customers and having a deep dialogue about them with your team, you can develop the intuition to go much faster in implementing any kind of innovation.

THE FORMATION OF CULTURE

When companies listen well and have internal alignment based around shared meaning, they can find their center of gravity and become more than just a participant in their marketplace. They can become a driver in the formation of culture. Nike is a great example. When they expanded into the golf market in 1995, with apparel, balls, and equipment, they used their successful formula of participating in a market at a level of deep understanding. Nike entered the market quietly. They developed a deep dialogue with club pros and top players, highlighted by the $100 million dollar sponsorship of Tiger Woods. Once they had the right relationships in the market, Nike went on a learning quest. They not only wanted to get to know the players, but also their needs on a deeper level. It took Nike four years to fully find their center of gravity, but by 1999 they had put all the pieces together and became the leader in a very competitive marketplace. That year, the winner of the British Open won the tournament in a pair of Nike shoes. Next, in 2000, Tiger Woods dropped his relationship with Titleist and started to play very successfully using Nike's new golf balls. The final piece fell into place when David Duval won his first major tournament in 2002 using Nike's new clubs. All of the hard work and deep dialogue around the needs of golfers started to pay off as they became a resounding market leader in a short period of time. Nike does more than participate in the sports marketplace; they understand their center of gravity as a brand so well that they help form the culture of sports. Like Nike, companies that can successfully communicate their understanding of their own center of gravity are usually industry leaders. Think about your industry. Does one company within it understand themselves, the marketplace and their customers so well that they dominate the competition?

Sometimes, however, internal cultures get in the way of listening and creating shared meaning. You've probably seen it in your company. Two vice presidents disagree on a course of action. Instead of

1) THEIR WORLD VIEW IS:

2) THEY ARE MORE ORIENTED TOWARD:

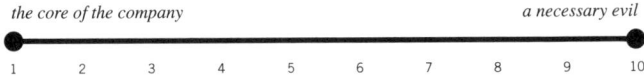

3) CUSTOMERS ARE PERCEIVED AS:

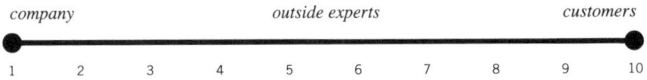

4) WHO IS RIGHT MOST OF THE TIME?

5) THEIR LISTENING IS GUIDED BY:

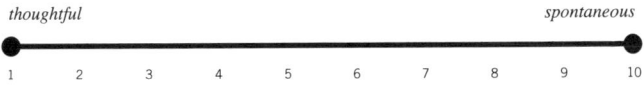

6) THEY ARE:

FIGURE 7.4 *Contextual Questions*

getting in a room, resolving their differences and moving on together, often one will encourage the project along while the other is subtly trying to put the brakes on it. Just like individuals, all organizations have their own filters and assumptions that over time harden into mental models of the world. These models act as a lens, or filter, that alters the way an individual or company sees the world. Factors that contribute to a lens include our individual expectations, beliefs, assumptions, values, history, and unwritten rules. The reality is that we all have filters that are permanently attached. We cannot walk away from our own childhoods and life experiences and their effect on the way we view the world. Likewise, a company cannot forget its own history. Ironically, many times companies that have been the most successful have the thickest lenses. Their own success has told them that the world works in a specific way. Hence, when the paradigm shifts they may be the last to notice. Successful companies must invest a great deal of effort to understand their lens and how it alters their perceptions of reality in the marketplace.

It is helpful to gain a deep understanding of each participant you work with in developing your company's bottom-up strategy, including individuals on your team and in your company, and the filters each brings to any interaction. To spark further thinking and dialogue regarding how individuals might act within the context of the community, consider asking yourself a few contextual questions (see Fig. 7.4). Keeping each participant in mind as you answer some key questions can help give both team and company members greater dimension; this in turn provides you with a better understanding of how they may interact with each other in the quest to find your center of gravity.

Our lenses can be helpful in determining our horizon of expectation and what we will accept as valid. However, large organizations often embed these mental models into their structure, dividing the world into categories. And from this static perspective, it can become very difficult to see or act upon opportunities that lie within the open space between and across categories. In rock climbing, finding the center of gravity is about knowing your environment and yourself well enough to predict how the combination of the two will best interact to accomplish your climb. Likewise in business, it not only means understanding the world around you, but also the internal world of your company.

The real goal in finding your center of gravity is to innovate. Innovation is always an act of courage, conviction and passion. With a firm grasp on your center of gravity and the internal alignment of your team, you will help engender these essential traits.

INTERNAL ALIGNMENT

With internal alignment around its center of gravity, a company can begin to evolve its interactions in the marketplace and drive real innovation. In Chapter Three we talked about the ecological term "ecotone." In a sense an ecotone is a natural center of gravity, a place where evolution is happening at a quick pace. Likewise, the center of gravity is the place where things are changing quickly, yet if you are centered, this change doesn't feel out of control. Remember, an ecotone is a place where two different, distinctive ecosystems meet. In this case, it represents the external ecosystem of the marketplace and the internal ecosystem of your company.

Too often the learning that's happening at the center of gravity never gets fully communicated to the core of a company, where significant changes to the soul or philosophy of a company really happen. The key is to understand and communicate the inspiration throughout an organization in a powerful way.

THE GRAVITY OF CREATIVITY

When I'm climbing and having a difficult time finding my center of gravity, many times I try to change my focus and think creatively about the situation. Often in climbing, it's easy to get overly focused on the goal of completing the climb, instead of thinking creatively about the more immediate situation that you're in. In some cases, the only way to the top is to go sideways or sometimes down to find a new, creative solution to the problem. Sometimes it means trying to use your body in a new way, like hooking your heel on a hold above your head, and using your hamstring as a bicep, pulling the rest of your body up, finding a new center of gravity.

Likewise in business, creativity must be employed to get a sense of the center of gravity. By creativity, I mean getting away from the preciousness of having to get everything right. It means getting everyone on the team to start thinking about finding the center of gravity more as a process than a goal. Corporate annual reports routinely proclaim a commitment to creativity and innovation, yet these traits rarely show up anywhere else in the company. In some companies, creativity and innovation are philosophical concepts, rather than practical direction. Too often, creativity and innovation are sought out but never understood, and never incorporated into a working, evolving strategy. Conversely, innovation can also be so incremental and predictable that it isn't really innovation at all. I'm talking about going beyond just encouraging creativity, and about developing a process that makes creativity an active part of the bottom-up strategy you follow. Here are some ideas to spur creativity in the pursuit of the center of gravity:

- **Introduce Conflicting Viewpoints** – The first step in implementing this kind of creativity is to expose the people you work with to a variety of conflicting perspectives. It's important and valuable for people to realize there are many ways to look at a problem.

- **Encourage Raw Ideas** – Get in the habit of bringing radical new ideas to the table. Every time your internal team gets together, take five minutes and ask for the most creative idea, no matter how crazy. Support it with a rotating award.

- **Reduce Resources** – Try giving your team fewer resources and see what happens. Be sure to give them more time to do things themselves. Instead of hiring someone else to lead a meaning-making session in the quest of finding your center of gravity, experiment with doing it yourself. It's okay to make mistakes and get frustrated with the process. That's all part of the game. The key is that you and your team are learning.

- **Facilitate an Institutional Memory** – In your quest to find the center of gravity, make sure that the process is documented and shareable. It's not only important to share the findings and inspiration, but also the process. In order for a company to be positioned on the center of gravity it must have the capacity to learn as an organization. Remember to facilitate the ability of your team to share their experiences through stories. We'll talk more about this in Chapter Eight.
- **Allow Experimentation** – Another key to making meaning is to allow the process time to explore mistakes and dead ends. Too many companies are looking for the right answer instead of being open to seeing the environment as it is. As we discussed earlier, it's the difference between looking and seeing.
- **Use Short-Term Mentoring** – Seek out the people in the company who have a wealth of experience in meaning-making in the context of the environment you are exploring. Let your team use them as short-term mentors. Short-term could be a one-hour dialogue or a couple of days of learning.
- **Don't Be a Slave to Research** – How many times have you heard, "Well, that's what the research says" when you know that it just doesn't feel right? When you feel this way, take the time to dig deeper. If your gut tells you something is lacking, or just plain wrong, trust your instinct. Don't take anything at face value. Go slower and farther in locating the real center of gravity. Then you can go faster in your innovation process.
- **Participate in Dialogue** – Earlier we talked about the difference between dialogue and discussion. While discussion usually

leads people to hold separate points of view, dialogue can lead to shared meaning, the first step on the road to finding the center of gravity.

- **Change Environments** – All too often, teams get in the habit of holding a weekly meeting in the same room, using the same agenda, at the same time every week. While that's an efficient way to have a meeting, it's probably not the best way to inspire meaning making. Try to keep the creativity flowing by changing things up. Alternate the team member who runs the meeting weekly. Let them develop the agenda. Infuse creativity.

- **Offer Your Time and Energy** – In any company, whether it has ten or ten thousand people, it's critical that the leaders of the company and of individual teams are accessible and willing to give of their time and energy. Developing a culture of such generosity will yield enormous benefits in laying a foundation of trust, where creativity can flourish on the road to finding the center of gravity.

EVOLVE YOUR LANGUAGE

How does your team talk about the learning you've been discovering from your bottom-up strategy? You can learn a lot about a company by the language people use to describe how they engage with their customers and the marketplace. Do you use the latest business jargon, or is it an organic language grown out of the evolution of your company? The language of a company pursuing an evolved strategy, not surprisingly, reflects its immediate environment. For instance, Nike uses the language of sports, while Intel uses the language of technical innovation. The language must also be a tool to promote creativity in the pursuit of finding the center of gravity. Here are some examples of language styles that can help promote creativity:

- **Raw** – Conversations in the pursuit of creativity and the center of gravity need to be honest and rugged. They also need to be in context. Too many times I've seen executives holed up in a four-star hotel, being catered to for their every whim, while focusing on finding the market's center of gravity. If you're trying to explore teens, go to a place where they might hang out. Invite a few of them to the meeting. Also, the rawness can come in when you let go of the corporate hierarchy in team meetings. This is a team in search of inspiration – not a couple of VPs, a few directors, and a handful of marketing people. In that situation, everyone sits there waiting to agree with one of the VPs. Make it accessible. Make it raw. Make it real.

- **Contradiction** – The world is full of contradiction, yet many companies would rather actively avoid it or pretend it doesn't exist. Support contradiction by exposing people to as many real perspectives as possible. To get to the center of gravity in a dynamic world, you need to understand the contradictions. Some of the best bottom-up strategies have subtle contradictory parts. Contradiction is a valid part of our lives and has a place in every process.

- **Collaboration** – I've found that company leaders – especially founders – can set the tone for how people behave toward one another. One important element of collaboration is generosity. Creating an atmosphere where ideas can be shared freely results in people being unafraid that someone will "steal" their ideas. Instead, they will engage with each other and create a deeper dialogue.

- **Dialogue** – As we discussed earlier, dialogue is a powerful tool. So many companies are either argumentative, having a power struggle between factions, or use discussion, a tool used in the classroom under the supervision of a professor, in the pursuit of the center of gravity. Dialogue focuses you on the journey and not the destination by rewarding collective effort. Dialogue is not a way of clubbing an idea to death. Instead, it's about finding a way to move the idea forward in a conclusive way. Many people in business situations confuse dialogue and discussion. The goal in a dialogue is for everyone to be in a different place when it is over. It's about evolution. The goal of a dialogue is to reach a place where no one asks a question to which he or she already knows the answer – a place where ideas move in one direction only: Forward.

- **Storytelling** – It's important to get your team together in a casual setting and swap stories. When storytelling, think about creative ideas that have succeeded and failed and unique solutions to especially difficult problems. Share everything from breakthroughs to breakdowns. The real purpose of such a gathering is to perpetuate institutional memory and knowledge.

Companies with no knowledge of their own oral history tend to borrow one to answer their own strategic questions. That's one of the reasons so much advertising today is interchangeable. Storytelling can be fostered by the design and flow of an organization's social and community habits, like its informal gatherings. Stories are a way of communicating. They offer a way of keeping the company true to its center of gravity.

FINDING THE CENTER OF GRAVITY

Finding the center of gravity means that you yourself are on a quest for the genuinely new, and that if you achieve that quest you will immediately start searching all over again. There's no goal when trying to understand your center of gravity. It's a journey. Once you find the center of gravity, it usually moves, unless you are standing still. It's all about evolving and exploring new terrain. Here are some ideas to help you along your journey:

- **Get Out** – Whether it's to hang out with a customer, see a retailer, or have a meeting, try getting out of the office and into the field so that you are in the same context as the dialogue you're having. It's always important to continue to reframe the dialogue by changing the environment.

- **Flex Your Intuition** – As discussed in Chapter 6, really flex your intuition. Encourage people to think about blue-sky scenarios. A good exercise is to start creating group stories. One person starts a story, and everyone else helps to finish it.

- **Hire the Right People** – The first step on this journey is to teach people inside a company to think about who the customers are as people, and then hire people who fit this profile. Many of the best young companies – for instance Nike, Patagonia, Burton, and Microsoft – have an innate, intimate knowledge of their customers' needs and preferences because they have taken the time and steps needed to relate to their customers. Beyond a certain point, company and customer come to share common values, sometimes deeply.

- **Discover a Corporate Sage** – Some people have a natural intuition. Usually these people are artists with a keenly developed sensuality. A prime example would be Tinker Hatfield, Nike's renowned design director. Hatfield is a great natural listener, and when you spend time with him, he has an instinctive ability to broaden the frame of the conversation. He is always asking "Why?" Perhaps it is not surprising, then, that inside Nike, Hatfield has become a sage. Every company needs to find people with the natural ability to be intuitive and help them become a corporate sage.

- **Evolve Your Philosophy** – Michael Jager, creative director of the Jager, DiPola, Kemp (JDK) advertising agency, sees the world differently than most. JDK operates with a manifesto at its core called "The Consciousness of Chaos." This manifesto describes how the world is changing and becoming incredibly fragmented. In order to respond to these rapid changes, Jager envisions a state where managing in the context of this chaos can be built upon "embracing fluid thinking without fear." Evolve your corporate philosophy so that it captures the center of gravity of the marketplace.

Remember, finding the center of gravity is critical for any company's adaptation and survival in the face of in this bottom-up economy. Such an environment demands participants that seek efficiency in the use of intelligence gathered from the community and its creative use in co-creating and driving innovation forward.

CHAPTER 8
Step Seven: Tell the Story

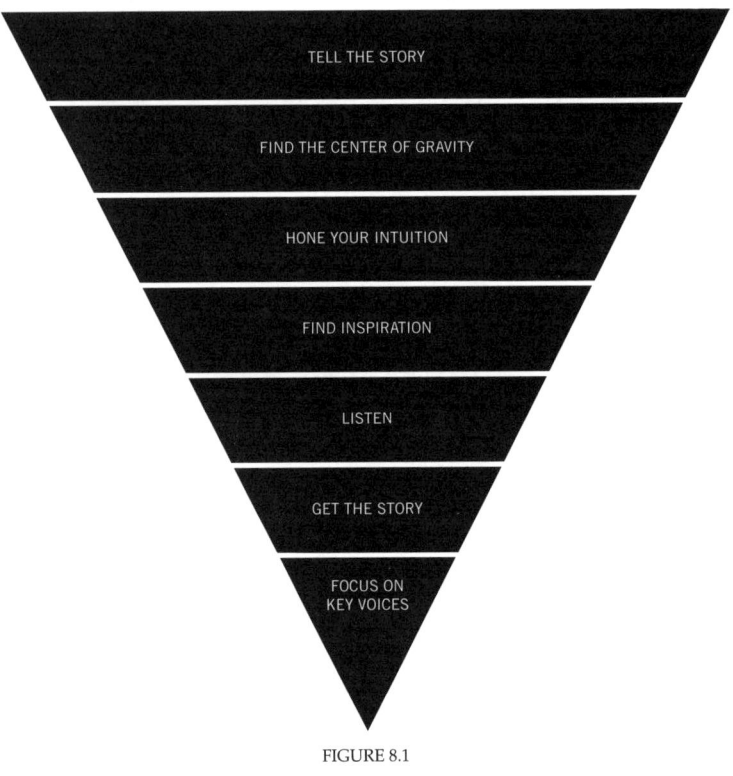

FIGURE 8.1

Storytelling is the most ancient form of sharing information known to man. Stories carry our hopes, dreams and values. They arouse our curiosity and invite us to wonder. They are also a gold mine for anyone trying to gain deeper knowledge. When told well, they stick in one's mind forever. Julie Taymor, the designer of the "Lion King" play, said, "It's how you tell the story that makes it new. That's what artists do. They let us look at the world from a different perspective. They let us look at birds in a way that makes us never see birds again in the same way."

WHY STORYTELLING?

Telling stories doesn't sound very business-like, does it? Especially when the typical way that most corporations look at their customers is through the rigid paradigm of analytical thinking. You know the drill: Analyze the customers, fix the systems, re-engineer the products. Everything can be laid out on a graph or a chart. Companies develop plans into which they try to fit an individual customer's needs as mechanically as they would analyze a computer bug. Step one… step two… step three. They then build elaborate mechanics to share the information, usually in the dreaded PowerPoint presentation. The reality is that traditional PowerPoint presentations are obscure, mechanistic, and lifeless. Charts and graphs communicate something very different from pictures of living things. Who hasn't sat through an awful PowerPoint presentation?

A couple of years ago I was at a conference where one of the featured speakers got up and clearly demonstrated the potential problems of using PowerPoint. The speaker was a well-known marketing strategist and author who specialized in teens and all things hip. When she first showed up, she sat near the door of the conference room, taking calls on her cell phone while the speaker at the podium had to repeat several sentences to be heard. To make matters worse, the obnoxious speaker opted to dress like the teenager she was scheduled to talk about, by wearing what looked like a size four miniskirt – when she really needed to be wearing a size ten. When she finally took the podium, she looked awkward in her very tight dress and disheveled blonde hair. Then, instead of engaging the audience, she used her forefinger to twist her hair while she chewed on it. Her presentation, created in PowerPoint, consisted of white slides with over 150 words on each in Times 12-point text. She proceeded to read her slides verbatim for the next half-hour, looking up from the screen of her laptop only long enough to chew a few more strands of hair. It didn't take long before most of the audience was dedicating their time to doodling or moving towards the door to find the restroom.

After the mechanistic analysis that businesses have applied to all of their strategic questions, the format used to present them isn't always much help. The problem is that these presentations don't deal with the complexity, clutter, and confusion of the reality and living inspiration from the customers. Analytical presentations rarely succeed in persuading companies to change in a profound enough way to find the market's center of gravity.

At the root of this analytical approach is the education many of us received at business school. When I was attending Denver University, there wasn't a lot of room for stories. Instead, there was a focus on statistically verifiable analysis that was provable. Statistically based tools poorly express the complexities of human needs in an easily understood fashion. Instead of speaking in the context of the corporate language, stories insist that we speak from human experience, allowing humanity into the strategic thinking process. Where the typical presentation about customers seeks to isolate and reduce, the story expands and encourages. Stories help exercise our imaginations.

Despite this apparent ignorance of narrative, storytelling is pervasive in all of our lives. Storytelling creates dialogue and brings a sense of continuity to our lives. It is an integral part of human communications. In fact, many scientists feel that storytelling is one of the most fundamental ways our brains are structured and how we relate experience. Everything we experience as humans involves telling and listening to stories. Movies, television, and the other mass media have been so successful because they are vehicles for storytelling. They transfer relevant information in a very fast and efficient format. When done well, these stories can become myths. When I saw the movie, "The Lord of the Rings: The Return of the King," I was surprised by how many people took the effort to dress in costume to come to the theater. "The Lord of the Rings" is a great story that resonates deeply and has become a myth through people's sharing of the story. Stories serve the purpose of helping us put information and experience in context. Great stories become myths by deeply resonating with their audiences, becoming the source of our thinking and culture.

Historically, stories have also been the most successful way for people and societies to store their most important information. Since ancient times, cultures have shared the meaning of human existence through storytelling. Likewise, companies remember their own cultures by the stories that are told and retold in the company's hallways. Think about powerful stories that are told inside your company. Is there a founding story? Is there a story of a brilliant strategic move? Stories bring context and meaning to the work we all do. They resonate deeply in our souls. One of the reasons that stories are so successful is that they mirror the way our minds work. They have always been at the center of our evolutionary communications and have been the main mechanism for passing on our values and principles from one generation to another.

So, if stories work so well at communicating complicated information, what kind of stories are the most successful in communicating inspiration from a company's center of gravity? They are stories that are told with a single voice. They explain the strategic question trying to be answered in a way that can be easily understood across the company, and also be familiar to the particular audience. You've got to know your audiences and tailor the story for each one. Lastly, the story must capture the imaginations of the audience by sharing some magic, while at the same time believable, so that it feels like a premonition of what the future could be like.

Inspirational stories must also be simple and as concise as possible. It's more important to spark new stories in the minds of the listeners, which they can invent in the context of their own environments, instead of sharing the details of exactly what happened in your intelligence gathering.

Last year, we worked with a client on trying to decipher their customers' behavior and how those customers might react to the launch of their brand into a new channel, at Wal-Mart. After spending several weeks with a handful of customers, one individual began to epitomize the prototypical customer and the challenges that the company would have in launching their product in Wal-Mart. During the investigation this customer, Heidi, began to represent the center of gravity. Heidi was a young, single mother living close to the poverty line and trying hard to support her family. We started asking each other, "What would Heidi think?" when we had a dialogue with our client regarding their strategy. The final presentation that was created to inform the senior management of the company was a series of stories about different customers and their lives. Most prominent within these stories was Heidi's. To ensure that everyone would grasp not only the story itself, but also deeply understand the context of Heidi's life, we used a great deal of video. Similar to many of our projects, Heidi was videotaped in her daily context: showing us her home and closet, driving around town, talking with others at a friend's house about their lives and, lastly, while shopping. In the final presentation we were able to immerse the senior executives in the context of Heidi's life. Today when there is a strategic issue that needs to be discussed in regards to Wal-Mart and the brand's customers, people still ask themselves, "What would Heidi think?" The strategy is now always compared to the center of gravity that is represented by Heidi.

It's always good when stories also have a happy ending. This makes it easier for listeners to make the leap from the explicit story being told, to the implicit story that is important to move the company forward.

The reality is that most strategic questions are so big now that they can feel unmanageable or incomprehensible. The magnitude can dwarf us as individuals, making us feel insignificant and giving us the impression that we have no ability to influence the issues. The very size of global strategic issues can lead to the feeling that it doesn't really matter what we as individuals might think. The strategic questions create their own dynamic that must be overcome before solutions can be found.

Storytelling is the best tool for dealing with the immenseness of such strategic issues, especially when trying to get the rest of the company to buy into a plan to move forward and innovate. These kinds of stories must provide a kind of plausibility, coherence, and reasonableness that enables people to make sense of the immensely complex issues that are being examined. A powerful story can hold the different elements of a strategic question together long enough to energize and inspire action. Such a story can give people the ability to make sense of whatever happens in the context of their own lives, allowing them to contribute their own input toward creating the future of the company.

For the story to be effective in sharing inspiration and driving innovation, it is more important that the story be true in the context of the company than be scientifically true. It is also important that the story be true in the sense of the narrative and the point of the story itself with its goal of inspiring change and innovation.

When the story resonates with the audience, it generates a new framework in their minds about the strategic question being asked. It is more important for the audience to be able to immerse themselves in the story than listen to the mere transmission of information. This immersion can have an impact far beyond the obvious and lead to the embodiment of the inspiration, much the way our client has put Heidi's face on their strategic quest discussed previously. By becoming immersed in a story, the audience is able to participate in the journey of finding the inspiration.

Most of the time listeners miss certain details in any presentation about this inspiration. In our dynamic world, the inspiration we have found by using a bottom-up strategy is not precise and is usually still evolving. This inspiration usually cannot be captured or even fully understood at a static point in time. Incompleteness of communication is a reality.

The goal of any presentation, whether dynamic or static, is to provoke inspiration that will feel new and self-generated by the listeners themselves. Inspiration can then become part of the way in which everyone internally sees his or her work. Ultimately, when people begin to form communities around the inspiration, and create a safe place to extend this inspiration into innovation, a presentation has succeeded.

To accomplish this, the story must take the audience on a virtual journey to the context of the story where it's actually happening, on the streets or in someone's home. This transition from physical to virtual worlds must happen actively so listeners are constantly inspired to co-create with the storyteller. Luckily, as humans, we seem to be able to slip in and out of the physical and virtual worlds with ease.

When fully engaged, the listeners can work with the storyteller to focus on generating the virtual world of the story. As the story unfolds, listeners can feel connected to not just the story itself but also to the participants in the story, the storyteller and their fellow listeners. The listener can momentarily be transported to view the world through the eyes of those in the story itself. Such a story can help them reframe their worldview in a profound way and become a common rallying cry around the center of gravity of the marketplace.

In contrast, when you listen to a presentation built on the foundation of static thinking instead of the foundation of a dynamic narrative, your mind is active in a very different way than when participating in a story. When (or if) engaged in listening to a presentation based on static thinking, the listener is not encouraged to call upon his or her own experience to make the presentation more relevant. Most of the time a listener has to put everything out of his or her mind and focus solely on understanding this static thinking. They are required to forget their own imaginations, experiences, and anything else that might be a distraction from the presentation. When listening to a story, the opposite happens. The listener must actively participate and contribute to the context of the story in his or her mind and, in effect, help tell him or herself the story. Such active participation promotes a common understanding, based on the experience of listening to the story, that the audience will continue to relate long after the exact details are forgotten.

The listener is invited to not only listen but to live the story with the storyteller, contextualizing into a living experience. Part of what makes a story successful is providing a place for the listener to visit on their virtual journey to further nurture their own experience.

Finding the center of gravity is one of the most critical issues for any company's adaptation and survival in the face of an increasingly dissonant environment. Such an environment demands participants that seek efficiency in the use of intelligence gathered from the marketplace and its creative use in driving innovation forward.

STORYTELLING VERSUS INSTRUCTION

While trying to use storytelling to spread inspiration throughout a company, avoid falling into the instructor mode. Your company doesn't need teachers who impart their knowledge to the uneducated; it needs co-creators of stories that spark creativity in their teammates. While stories can generate positive attitudes that will inspire innovation, instruction usually doesn't.

Listening to stories gives participants the space to fill in the gaps of the story and imagine the missing links in the context of their own work. The meaning of the story that you are trying to convey is usually not in the story itself, but instead in the meaning that the listeners help create out of the story. Finding the center of gravity means finding meaning in the story in the context of the listener's own work.

One of the biggest problems with the typical corporate presentation, concentrating on hard facts and findings, is that this static way of thinking leaves most people, on the outside of the process as spectators, self-conscious. It's as though they are watching the facts being presented on the other side of a glass wall, with no way to interact. Such a presentation is a static picture and has no way of making the dynamic intelligence come alive and be usable.

In contrast, storytelling and the narrative way of thinking are immersive and can be easily internalized. They demand that the listeners forget themselves and participate in the journey of finding the center of gravity. As David Abrams said in *The Spell of the Sensuous*, the explicit meanings of the actual words ride on the surface of this depth like the waves on the surface of the sea.

Somehow in our corporate lives our jobs have come to demand that we treat people as mechanical things. We've deceived ourselves into believing that we can be objective. Yet, when we are in a social setting with our friends we treat people very differently – as humans, not as things to be manipulated. The result of the mechanical behavior in most companies is that there is a breakdown in trust. Without such trust, not only with fellow employees but also with customers, it is impossible to find the elusive center of gravity.

In the effort to find the center of gravity and communicate it internally, the goal of storytelling is to facilitate the rearranging of established knowledge inside the company and encourages the listeners to make new connections between what they currently do and what they need to do to be centered. The ultimate goal is to encourage listeners to generate their own stories around the principals of the story you are communicating. A listener hears the storyteller's delivery of the story and, simultaneously, hears a silent voice within themselves, as their minds create a variety of outcomes to the story, built upon their own personal experiences. Instead of playing the role of the teacher, a storyteller should allow some mental space in the story for the listeners to forge their own thoughts. A good storyteller must keep in mind the objective of having listeners invent their own stories built on the foundation of the original story. When this mental space is offered, everyone in the audience can co-create in a way that bonds them deeply to a common experience.

Storytelling can also be considered an incredibly useful tool for coping with complexity. As humans, we have always used this narrative language as the most efficient way to communicate the nature and behavior of complex adaptive phenomena. As a description of complex systems, stories are considerably more accurate than scientific thinking. Our world is full of these systems. Look around. Anything that is important to know about – people, companies, economies, animals, plants and weather – is a complex system. Humans have always intuitively used stories to communicate the complexity that is all around us. This is why stories are ubiquitous. It is only when we try to get serious that our minds lock up, our business school mindsets take over, and we start talking in linear terms about complex phenomena and drawing two-dimensional maps of our thoughts.

DEVELOPING THE STORY

We are in the twilight of a society based on data. In the coming years, brands and companies will not thrive on the basis of their data, but on the strength and meaning of their stories, creating products and services that evoke emotion. Products will become less important than the stories they convey and the way those stories are interpreted. It is a return of the ancient form of narrative. Companies need to have stories to tell that inspire action and embody those stories with congruency and authenticity.

When developing your story, there are some essential qualities your narrative must have:

- **Context** – The story must be in the context of the audience's experience. You want the audience to think about their own experiences and stories and be able to see themselves in the story.

- **Simplicity** – I'm sure you've been in a meeting where someone starts telling a story that gets so complicated and long that everyone gets lost. I always try to keep each slide in my presentation to no more than two sentences. Sometimes the simplicity of one word is even more powerful. When trying to explain something like the meaning of a term, it's not necessary to give a paragraph-long explanation. Show the word and talk about the meaning. Keep your story simple and to the point.

- **Interest** – We've all sat through presentations where it seems as though the presenter has lost his or her way. You can look around and see the audience wander off with the speaker and tune out the rest of the presentation. Engage the audience with an interesting story. If it's boring, the story will do nothing to inspire action or promote understanding. A story has to be interesting enough for the audience to register, remember, and tell it again.

- **Trust** – The best stories are true. I don't mean true in a scientific context, but true to the audience's experience. It's amazing the trust that is created when you feel the audience saying that they've been in the same situation. True stories evoke an attitude of "I can do it, too."

- **Meaning** – A story must get across a strong message that inspires the audience to rethink something. The story is the framework that adds support to the deeper message being conveyed. It's easy to get lost in the story itself and forget why you are telling it. Remember that a story is not just a way to illustrate the analysis, rather to convey meaning and act as a conduit of understanding.

- **Connectedness** – To be successful, the story must connect the audience with the inspiration you are trying to convey and to customers with whom the audience can empathize. It is vital to get the listeners to mentally place themselves in the shoes of the customers.

- **Magic** – A great story often violates the listener's expectations. There is a surprise. This gift is usually an action that has resulted in laying the groundwork for profound inspiration in the story. Remember to plant the seed of the idea of the center of gravity and let them invent the missing elements.

- **Relevance** – A successful story must embody the inspiration in such a way that the audience will almost intuitively know what to do with it. If the listeners are given the opportunity to co-create the story, they will believe that it is their story and will more likely become champions of the inspiration you are trying to share.

- **Immediacy** – Stories are efficient. When the deadline is tight, it isn't possible to detail all of the data to scientifically prove your point. A story helps people take the leap of faith necessary to innovate.

Remember, the goal of a bottom-up strategy is to catalyze organizational change around the center of gravity in the marketplace. Stories play an important role in making this happen.

SHARING THE STORY

In order for an organization to really change, inspiration from the street must find its way into the core of the company. As in any other organism, change happens at the fringes of a species. The center of the species is always the last to change and the part of the community that resists change the most. It is essential to take the intelligence found on the streets and start a revolution internally. That means making that intelligence as impactful as possible. Impact can come from ease of use, accessibility, insight, relevance and beauty. But the real power resides in the actual presentation of the story. It is also essential to remember that you are simply the storyteller, the illustrator of the information, and that the story itself should be the star. Your job is to be the conduit between the intelligence from the streets and the rest of the company.

Here are some things to think about when you're sharing your stories, to make them as impactful as they can be:

- **Engage the Audience** – While a great story can engage the audience, most of the time the magic comes from the way it is told. Think about reading stories with your parents when you were a kid. The best stories were those that your parents were passionate about and told with excitement. As a speaker, if you're excited by what you're talking about, chances are your audience will be excited as well. Conversely, if you dread the story you are telling, then your audience will too. Think about how you can get excited to tell the story. Be passionate.

- **Ownership** – To motivate people through storytelling, you must master the performance of the story. By mastering the story you can free yourself to have the flexibility to deal with even the most difficult situations. I was speaking at a "Voice of the Customer" conference, and went to the podium to turn on my computer and set up for the telling of my story as the audience was having lunch. For some reason, my computer crashed and would not turn on. A couple of days before, I had made a CD of my presentation, but in the 48 hours before the speech I had changed the material radically. Fortunately, someone loaned me a computer and I was able to use the CD to rebuild the story in a half hour. The only way I was able to pull it off was because I knew the material so well that I could retype several slides from memory. I owned the story.

- **Testing** – You know the saying: Practice makes perfect. There is no substitution for it. Focus your energies on the core of the story, making it interesting and meaningful in the story's presentation. Practice in front of people and get feedback. Don't be afraid to modify the story up till the very end. I always find the more times I practice a story, the more small changes I make to it. The story becomes my story. Only then can the magic of ownership really come out.

- **Informal Settings** – I always find that if you're relaxed as a storyteller, then your audience will also be relaxed. One of the ways to make the setting more informal is to start the story off with a series of questions. Solicit participation in the story's co-creation. Every once in a while slow down, take a breath and ask more questions. It keeps the audience engaged and the setting more informal. It becomes a dialogue between peers instead of a classroom setting where a teacher instructs the students.

SUPPORTING AND SPREADING YOUR STORY

Your stories can be greatly enhanced with the use of strong visual and audio tools. Video is definitely the strongest way to share a story; by which I mean a video that follows the storytelling guidelines discussed above. There's no way that 20 hours of bad focus group video will do anything to support your point. Short of using video, the next best thing is photography, preferably images that are as gritty and real as possible. Remember, a quick snapshot of a real situation is always more powerful than any stock image. You want the viewer to feel as if they are there. So, document your point of view with a digital or disposable camera.

Lastly, think about the design of your story, whether it's written or delivered as a full presentation. We've all seen PowerPoint presentations that are a nightmare, but they don't have to be. Setting your presentation up in a creative way will allow for creativity as you tell the story. My rule is to never have more than one sentence per slide. Don't talk directly from the slides, but rather use them as reinforcement for your story. Likewise, when your story is written, design the document so that it feels light and inviting. Here are some things to remember when your presentation is being prepared:

- **Create Mental Space** – Great storytelling creates mental space for the audience to think and co-create. Build these spaces into the presentation of your story by leaving some white space. In written form that might mean putting only a few words on each page; when telling the story it might mean taking a deep breath and pausing for the audience to reflect, and in PowerPoint it might mean using fewer words per slide, and not trying to explain everything explicitly.

- **Allow Co-creation** – By creating mental space for the audience you are inviting them to co-create with you. The storyteller soliciting input will also enhance co-creation. Asking for participation is always a catalyst for co-creation. Even in a printed report, you can solicit participation with a few good questions.

- **Be Provocative** – Push the envelope. Try new things. If your company's standard practice is to tell stories in a memo created in a Word document, change it up. Add some photos. Pull out some meaningful quotes and feature them in larger type or a different font. Challenge the status quo and get people to want to read your story. If you really want to shake things up, use video. I can't stress to you enough that video is the most powerful way to share stories from the street. When you tell someone's story in a presentation, it can have some impact; if your customer is allowed to tell their own story via video, then you've captured the real world and have given people inside your company the ability to share some of this inspirational magic. Keep it real.

About the Author

John Winsor is CEO and co-founder of the ad agency Victors & Spoils, established in 2009 to be the first such agency built on crowdsourcing principles. Before that he was VP/Executive Director of Strategy and Innovation at Crispin, Porter + Bogusky, and prior to that he was the founder of Radar Communications and Sports & Fitness Publishing. He is also the author of *Spark* (Agate B2, 2010) and co-author with Alex Bogusky of *Baked In* (Agate B2, 2009).